TRAVERSE CITY, MICHIGAN

A Historical Narrative

1850-2013

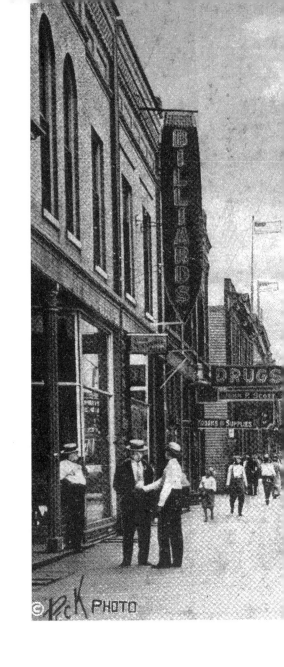

TRAVERSE CITY, MICHIGAN

A Historical Narrative

1850-2013

RICHARD FIDLER

Mission Point Press
2554 Chandler Lake Road
Traverse City MI 49696
missionpointpress.com

ISBN: 978-1-943995-40-0
Library of Congress Control Number: 2017950214

Printed and bound in the United States
First printing, 2013

Cover and book design by Saxon Design, Inc., Traverse City, MI

Published by Horizon Books, Traverse City, Michigan
www.horizonbooks.com

Printed in the United States of America.

Contents

Introduction

A general history of anything is an impossible undertaking. First, it is impossible to know enough about the uncountable number of topics that must be addressed. Second, it is impossible to winnow out the wheat from the chaff—to decide which topics are worthy of inclusion and which should be left out. Third, it is nearly impossible to avoid a monotonous recitation of facts and figures, dates and places, names and events, those things that go into a typical textbook or encyclopedic telling of history. History should never be boring: that would be an insult to those who acted it out.

It is, indeed, impossible to know everything about the history of a region. For nearly a decade I have searched through primary sources and secondary—impressing my print on the chair in front of my favorite microfilm reader at the public library as I examined old newspapers. The *Polk Directories* (describing residential and commercial Traverse City) provided endless hours of enjoyable study. Visits to the Bentley Historical Archives in Ann Arbor and to the State Archives in Lansing brightened a few days. Regional histories, articles in magazines, interviews with knowledgeable people—all of those broadened my understanding of the area. And nowadays, who cannot keep away from primary sources and internet websites? Best of all were lively discussions with my tiny history club, the Backspacers.

Still, the effort was not sufficient. Many topics in this book were addressed with a single authoritative source rather than a variety of sources. For example, the history of the National Music Camp and the Interlochen Arts Academy is best described in Dean Boal's book, *Interlochen, Home of the Arts*. A reader can tell if a book avoids bias and rests on a solid research foundation. Boal's book certainly qualified as a reliable source under those criteria. The

Front Street in the 1890s

present book will not be treasured for its scholarship: It lacks a true bibliography and footnotes or endnotes are nowhere to be found. Instead of those nods to academic correctness, there is a Resource Guide (Appendix C) for the study of local history at the end of the book, an effort to share sources with readers who may wish to begin their own local history investigations. After all, history is about seeking answers to questions—at least from my perspective—and what better way to launch those investigations than describing pathways I have walked in my own historical travels?

With regard to the problem of completeness, I confess to subjective judgment: I chose only those topics that seemed important to me. Throughout all chapters (except the last) I identified thematic organizers: *Challenges, Responses,* and *Changes. Challenges* refers to the questions and concerns of the time. In the first period of white settlement pioneers cared about taming the wilderness, attracting new settlers, and bringing "civilization" to a neglected part of the world. The next generation cared about industrialization, rather than physical survival, and set about to build factories and to grow the city.

Earlier concerns were not forgotten—only the emphasis changed. And so it went in years to come with each generation addressing its own challenges.

Accordingly, people made responses to those challenges—or not. Traverse City made enormous strides towards industrialization at the turn of the twentieth century, while neglecting the welfare of the local Indian community. Later in the thirties and forties, it responded to environmental degradation of the Boardman River with the construction of a sewage treatment plant, while neglecting to control growth with a sensible city plan. In this book, the thematic organizer *Responses* examines the measures taken to address the challenges described earlier, remembering that sometimes no effective response was made at all. Sometimes, if the response can be disposed of quickly, it is included within the *Challenges* section.

Whether or not effective responses were made to challenges, the area changed, each generation moving closer to the Traverse City we know today. Under the thematic organizer, *Changes,* I summarize those changes in a few paragraphs. Here again, I pretend no objectivity. Another person might look at the same collection of observations and draw different conclusions. But... isn't that the fun of history?

As for complaints that general histories are boring, I can only offer this admonishment taken from a sign in a Colorado saloon. Though it describes a pianist, it could also describe this historian: *Don't Shoot the Pianist. He is Trying His Best.*

Indeed, he is. One effort to capture the readers' interest was to provide a narrative description of Traverse City, imagining the smells, sights, and sounds of a particular place and time. The descriptions are as accurate as I could make them, drawing upon newspaper articles, historical photographs, and first-person accounts. Sometimes they are not based upon local evidence but upon information from outside sources. We know, for example, that Donati's Comet (described in Chapter One) was the brightest comet of the century and we know where it appeared in the sky. It took only a jump of imagination to have it reflected on the calm waters of the Bay in 1858. Did it actually appear as described? We don't know. The first edition of the local newspaper, the *Grand Traverse Herald*, appeared a month after its brightest display and there was no mention there.

I attempted to organize the book by giving a nod to chronology with each chapter representing thirty or forty years and by identifying the themes *(Challenges)* that permeated every generation. Throughout the book I did not include a storehouse of names, dates, places, and events because I was worried that the pianist might get shot. It is not that they aren't important. It is simply that the story could be told without them.

However, for those readers who ask for a skeleton of events and dates to hang their understanding of history upon, I offer a brief chronology in Appendix A. Its contents are arbitrary in the sense that I chose only those things that were meaningful to me.

To provide a glimpse into the evolution of Traverse City in the twentieth century, I present selected aerial photographs taken in twenties, forties, fifties, and sixties in Appendix B. Peg Sicilliano and Maddie Buteyn assembled this collection, which is a part of a larger archive held by the History Center of Traverse City. They graciously allowed me to use captions they wrote for a recent exhibition at the History Center.

In addition to Peg Sicilliano's kind help with all sorts of questions, Dave Pennington, also at the History Center, tirelessly copied images onto a flash drive that eventually found their way onto these pages. The good people at the University of Michigan's Bentley Historical Archives directed me towards early Hannah-Lay records over the course of a pleasant day in Ann Arbor. Reference librarians at the Traverse Area District Library went beyond performing their ordinary duties in locating historical sources. Ann Swaney, reference librarian of Northwestern Michigan College, located pictures of the founding of that institution. I am especially grateful for the assistance of Marlas Hanson in examining the manuscript for errors, lapses in style, and occasional mistakes in historical content and interpretation. However, all remaining errors are mine, not hers. Thanks to all who participated in informal interviews and discussions, especially the Backspacers whose members offered encouragement, easy conversation, and cheerful acceptance of my occasionally unbalanced excitement over some aspect of historical trivia.

View of West Bay looking across the Boardman River, about 1861

CHAPTER ONE

The Traverse Settlement: 1850-1880

The Settlement: October, 1858

Exposed to stiff north winds off Grand Traverse Bay, a few forlorn buildings stood upon the sandy shore, surrounded by a disharmony of tree stumps. They were haphazardly arranged, without the grace and order imposed by a grid of streets, placed unskillfully as if by a young child in play. A few cottages, a general store, a boarding house, a simple frame building that housed the *Grand Traverse Herald* newspaper, two rude hotels, a doctor's office and residence, and a school house well back from the waterfront expressed the tenuous hold civilization exerted upon this wild and beautiful place. A few other buildings dotted the area, some made of barked slabs from the nearby mill: they offered survival rather than the dignity of a well-kept home.

There were two mills: that erected upon Mill Creek by Horace Boardman more than a decade previous and the coal-fired Hannah and Lay mill that occupied a space nearly at the center of the settlement between the Boardman River and the Bay. They performed the dirty work that brought men here: the reduction of logs to boards intended for the construction of buildings both near and far. The steam-powered mill poured black smoke over the Bay—at least when the wind blew from the south, keeping sparks away from the settlement. It was a fortunate happenstance, given the raging fires at the peak of the logging era to come.

The Hannah and Lay mill defined the sensory world of the settlement's inhabitants. The working of its saws cut the stillness of the air, allowing only the cries of gulls and crows to penetrate. The smell of sawdust was especially strong in the rainy days of spring. When the mills were busy, the Boardman River was full of logs, branches, and sawdust, its formerly clear and cold waters now brown and full of sediment and waste. From the assaults made by the sawmill upon the river, fish had begun to die, their bodies decaying along the banks. By its very smell, settlers did not get their water from the mouth of the river.

They did not lament the aggrieved waters of the river and the tortured land of stumps because there was an inexhaustible supply of untouched places nearby. South of the Boardman River white and red pines grew more than a hundred-fifty feet high, their sturdy trunks growing solitary without the confusion of understory trees. Here was the pinery: the forest that brought men with their axes to this part of the world. A soft layer of pine needles covered the forest floor, forming soft mulch that forbade the invasion of grass and weeds. In the pinery the harshness of the northern climate was muted: the wind was mostly calm under the distant canopy above, the sun only speckled the ground in summer and winter, and temperatures did not swing wildly between day and night as they did on the exposed beaches nearby.

At first the activities of the loggers seemed puny in the face of the grand elegance of the pine forest. Axes made only gradual progress in converting the stillness of the forest into the sunny and noisy plain close to the shacks that marked civilization's toehold upon the Bay. At night the howls of wolves kept settlers to home for fear of attack—if not from the roving packs then from bears that occasionally robbed a farmer of his prize sow. Men did not go out at night because light was a precious thing: kerosene lamps were unknown and oil lamps and candles were not to be used profligately.

Along with its terrors, the night offered its beauty. Without the intrusion of man-made light, the Milky Way spread across the sky, reflected on the Bay on the calmest of nights. The Dippers hung over the water, visible summer and winter, a sign post to lands further north. Anyone who went to the water's edge and stared up was rewarded with the flash of a meteor, sometimes a whole shower of them if the moon the hour and sky all combined to provide the right setting. Then there was Donati's comet, the brightest comet of the nineteenth century, which arrived in 1858.

To the settlers of the Traverse settlement, it was magnificent, draping over the Bay near the Big Dipper. It was at its brightest in early October when the sky was black, the moon new. Lincoln spoke of it when he was preparing for what would be known as the Lincoln-Douglas debates. It appeared in magazine illustrations and paintings of the time. At a time when city skies were mostly dark at night, it was visible to all, especially to those living in a small settlement facing north over a broad band of open water, Traverse City. Its presence anchored people's consciousness in Nature about them, both awesome and terrible. Its transience foreshadowed the end of Nature to come.

Challenges

In 1858 the overwhelming challenge for settlers was to fashion a safe and prosperous community from a natural world that was not always kind and forgiving. Winds blew cold in the winter here, and if they were warmer than in nearby places, it was only by comparison to the extreme bitterness farther north and east. Soils, especially where the pines were cleared, were sandy and poor, unsuitable for many crops such as corn. Upon the destruction of the forests, slash was burned on site, consuming what little humus had accumulated since the retreat of the ice only eight thousand years before. Frosts regularly occurred into late May, making for a short growing season. Biting insects ruled the late spring, sending outdoorsmen to open places exposed to the wind and sun.

In 1858 Traverse City was isolated in ways most other cities in the United States were not: it was situated at the end of a long peninsula, a fact that would shape its destiny over the next century and a half. At the end of a peninsula travelers are not on the way to any other destination. Roads do not pass

Schooner laden with lumber

through such places at first, especially if surrounding land is covered with impenetrable swamps, towering forests, steep hills, plunging valleys, and rivers needing to be bridged. The expense of building them is too great—and what would be the point of constructing them in the first place if they do not lead anywhere?

Traverse City made do without a road to southern Michigan until 1869, when the Northport-Newaygo road was finally completed. By that date the Oregon Trail leading across the country had existed for decades. Only two hundred fifty miles from Detroit, Traverse City was more isolated from the currents of civilization than small towns in Nebraska or Utah. Indian mail carriers regularly brought packages and letters from more civilized places in the south. The confirmation of Lincoln's death had to wait for a whole week before it was printed in the *Grand Traverse Herald* at a time when most of the rest of the country was covered with a telegraphic system that informed the population immediately.

The account of state legislator Perry Hannah underscores the isolation of Traverse City:

> When the legislature adjourned, early in the spring, some of the members came and shook hands with me and said, "I suppose you have to go on to your home all the way by stage." This was very amusing to me, coming from state legislators, when I knew my trip had to be made 'afoot and alone' through the long woods.

As with roads, railroads came slow to the area. When the transcontinental railroad was finished in 1869, Traverse City was still unconnected to the national railway system. In terms of attracting new residents, it was at a disadvantage since the railroad provided a cheap means of transporting goods and passengers to and from large population centers. In 1873, with the railroad in place, Traverse City residents were only thirteen hours from Chicago, a trip easily completed in a day. Even living in the heart of wilderness, Traverse residents could enjoy the concerts, exotic foods, shows, museums, and libraries of one of the world's fastest growing cities after only a day's travel.

With its connection to the Great Lakes, Traverse City should have enjoyed the advantages of transportation by boat. To some extent it did, but in the early years Grand Traverse Bay was thought to be dangerous to navigate,

Indian encampment at the mouth of the Boardman River

full of uncharted shoals and rocks. With those uncertainties captains had second thoughts about sailing all the way to its southern end. In time, this prejudice was overcome and the city did develop its port facilities, both for passenger ships and for freight. That said, travel by boat did have its problems.

First, it was slower than the railroads. By sail, a trip to Chicago depended on favorable winds, often taking two days or more, though steamboats could complete the journey in 24 hours. Second, as the ice of winter closed in, shipping ceased. In the middle of the nineteenth century, Grand Traverse Bay would typically freeze in February, not opening up until April or even later. Third, there was the omnipresent danger of shipwrecks. At a time when weather forecasting was in its infancy, violent storms appeared suddenly and shipwrecks took lives even into the twentieth century.

Beyond taming the wilderness, settlers had a more exalted goal: bringing civilization to a region that greatly needed it. Schools were required for the young, churches for those of faith, libraries for the edification of all, and a newspaper to inform residents of the news. After the trees were cut down, the land itself was to be civilized with the tilling of fields and husbanding of cattle, the construction of fences and barns, and the building of mills, factories, and other edifices of a wealthy society. Resources were to be used for human purposes for Nature was the servant of Man. The goal of civilizing the raw country was in the sight of the immigrants as they streamed north into wilderness. In their hearts they knew it would be fulfilled. Was their certainty the basis for the unbounded optimism of the late nineteenth century?

Responses

With its biting wintry cold, its frequent summer droughts, its predatory insects, its isolation from civilization, at first the Grand Traverse region attracted few settlers. Farmers would find better land in warmer, more southerly climes, where rainfall was more plentiful, the soil richer, the markets closer to population centers. Manufacturers could build factories close to the arteries of transportation, both roads and rails. College towns grew up near population centers, mining towns prospered wherever minerals were to be found, cities like Chicago and St. Louis were jumping off places for the great American West. With such competition, who would come to the rude settlement of Traverse City?

Some did not have to travel: they lived there. In 1858 local Indians were in a time of transition as the old ways of living in wigwams, preparing and eating traditional foods, wearing clothes made of buckskin, observing traditional courtship and marriage customs, speaking the Anishnaabe language were passing away. The settlement kept alive at Old Mission Peninsula by Reverend Peter Dougherty had moved to Omena in present-day Leelanau County a few years before. Many Indians had embraced Christianity to some extent, melding traditional belief in the Great Spirit with the Christian God, though beliefs in local spirits and ceremonies honoring the dead were not forgotten. Arriving from England in 1858 as a child, local painter William Holdsworth remembered encountering an Indian on Old Mission peninsula who communicated with sign language because he could not speak English. Within a generation or two Indian children would lose the ability to speak their native language.

Local Indians kept a low profile at this stage in their history. The Grand Traverse area was never a tribal center, that honor belonging to Michilimackinac at the tip of the lower peninsula (today's Mackinaw City). Less than a hundred years previously, several thousand Indians lived south of the Straits in miles of longhouses overlooking the shore of Lake Michigan. Largely because of disease brought by white settlers—spread both by accident and on purpose—that population shrank dramatically. Where before there were thousands, by 1858 there were only hundreds. Poverty, alcoholism, and despair accompanied the diminished population.

Still, the Indian presence touched those who inhabited the Traverse settlement in many ways. Indian drumming and dancing were known to all in the white community. Indians served as guides for the long trips to the more civilized lands of southern Michigan; they served as mail carriers; they worked in the logging industry; they comprised a regiment of sharpshooters dispatched to Civil War battlegrounds. Along the strip of beach where the Boardman River empties into West Bay, they set up camp in the summer, selling and trading goods with sailors and inhabitants of the settlement. Photographs dating from as late as the 1890's confirm the existence of summer encampments upon the beach.

The relationship of whites to Indians in the middle of the nineteenth century had lost the edge of hostility that characterized it a half century before. Indians were largely isolated from the currents of white civilization, the children rarely receiving more than a few years of education in mission schools. In trade and religion the two cultures mingled, often to the detriment of Indian traditions.

Logging enabled the Traverse settlement to survive. Mostly temporary residents, the loggers employed by Hannah and Lay varied in background and national origin. Some were farmers trying to earn money during the cold months of winter. Others were professionals who moved from camp to camp according to the possibilities for making the most money and getting the best camp food. Many came from Canada, moving west and south as the forests of the East gave up their timber. Certain ethnic groups migrated towards logging and work in sawmills: the French, the Irish, Germans, and in the Upper Peninsula especially, the Scandinavians. Mostly, they did not settle in the Traverse community, moving to the north and west as the trees came down locally.

Those with responsible jobs at the Hannah Lay Company, the bookkeepers, shopkeepers, and bosses, often stayed in the area. Perry Hannah and Albert Tracy Lay, two owners of the company, were two of them. At first, they alternated, one staying in Chicago for the year, the other in Traverse City, but as time passed, Hannah resolved to stay behind in the primitive village he had helped to create. Of course, Chicago was barely a day away by steamship so his sacrifice was not as great as might be imagined.

Local historian Robert Wilson compiled biographies of prominent settlers of the Grand Traverse area from the beginning of white settlement. Of the 26 described in the first volume of his *Grand Traverse Legends*, most were born in the United States with fully 14 coming from upstate New York, four with connections to other New England states, three with English-Scottish roots, and two from Canada. They were predominantly Protestant and voted

Republican in national elections, overwhelmingly choosing Abraham Lincoln over his Democratic opponent, Stephen Douglas. Newer waves of migrants would come from those places as well as Ohio, Lower Michigan, neighboring states, and—in large numbers—from Bohemia, the present Czech Republic.

Why did they come to Traverse City? Surely there was the prospect of creating a better life in a wilderness rich in natural resources. "Go west, young man!" was a slogan that did not point the adventurous towards the Rocky Mountains and beyond. In the first half of the nineteenth century it referred to lands west of the Appalachian Mountains—even the forested regions adjacent to the Great Lakes.

For the most part, immigrants were not informed about the land, the climate, and the living conditions of the Traverse area. Still, they came—some by serendipity—and some for reasons that influence new arrivals today: inexpensive land for farming, the beauty of water and forest, the freedom that goes with isolation from large population centers, and a sense of community created by individuals who must struggle together to earn a living. Seen this way, the chief disadvantage to living in Northern Michigan—its isolation—becomes its chief asset. However, Traverse City would have to promote this asset vigorously as it sought to increase its population and its wealth. Its success varied throughout its history.

Bohemians came to Traverse City at a very early date, the first families arriving in 1855. It is not clear why they came to Northern Michigan, since other regions more accessible by train and wagon were open for settlement. An intriguing coincidence is that most immigrants came through Chicago, the corporate headquarters of Hannah Lay. Is it possible that Perry Hannah or A. Tracy Lay recruited them to live in the newly created village at the foot of Grand Traverse Bay? We may never know, but whatever the reason for their coming, Bohemians left a mark on the community. Names of villages, streets and businesses reflect their presence: Greilick, Petertyl, Wilhelm, Kyselka, Kratochvil, and Schopieray.

Where did people meet in early Traverse City? In winter, they met nowhere. Here is a remembrance of an early settler, Thomas T. Bates:

> In 1862 there were but few forms of diversion or recreation available in Traverse City. Everyone was too busy with the sterner duties of life to engage in pleasuring. Occasionally, during the winter season, a sleigh-ride was indulged in, and a dance at

Early photograph of town founders, from left: A. Tracy Lay, James Morgan, Perry Hannah, William Morgan

the stopping place, but there was very little of that sort of social intercourse. Nearly all of the men were employed by Hannah, Lay & Co. in mill or store, and the women were too worn out with the day's struggle to keep these men fed and supplied with actual necessaries of life to care much for pleasure. Where everyone saw everyone during the day, there was no special inducement to play at meeting each other "socially."

The Hannah Lay store was a social center as well as a distributor of goods. We have a record of patrons and their purchases for the years 1857-59. According to the shop ledger, the store sold both everything and nothing. It offered hay bales, hardware, tallow, salt pork, flour, spices, woolen shirts, socks, tallow, tobacco, and yards of several kinds of cloth. On the other hand, it offered little choice to customers and provided mostly the "necessaries" of life rather than extravagances, a fact noted by the store's few women customers. Unsurprisingly, in this logging community most customers were males, many seeking a pair of socks or a plug of tobacco.

On average two-dozen customers would show up daily to make their sundry purchases. Even during the Christmas season business did not improve notably, whether from poverty or from custom. A few customers chose a pound or two of "nuts," possibly in celebration of the season, and a few women bought cinnamon and nutmeg for holiday baking and yards of cloth for sewing projects. On the whole, "Christmas shopping" was a phenomenon not yet in full flower. The fact that Christmas Day had only begun to be accepted as a general holiday across the United States may explain why the store was open on Christmas day, 1857.

It is not surprising that Christmas was not celebrated that year, since churches had not yet arrived at the settlement. Though Peter Dougherty's Presbyterian mission provided a religious outpost for the Indians, white settlers and loggers attended services only occasionally when itinerant preachers visited unexpectedly. Instead of religious services, various individuals from the community provided a sketch of ceremony for funerals and other major life events.

The absence of a religious community heightened the isolation of year-around residents starved for social contact during the interminable winters. One of the first pastors describes the celebration of Christmas from his point of view:

> The first Christmas formally observed in Traverse City was in the year AD 1859. For real pleasure and enjoyment we doubt whether it has ever been surpassed. Each seemed to vie with the other in the presentation of their highest testimonials of mutual love and regard. Mr. H.D. Campbell, then a sprightly youth and Miss Adsit played the role of "Grandparents." Little Marcella Steele was their "Granddaughter" and Dr. Goodale was acting "Santa Claus". The writer of the sketch (the author of this description) was surprised with the presentation of a live turkey festooned and trimmed for the occasion and a purse of gold containing $107.50.

Like the store, the church was a center for social activity. Methodists, Baptists, Congregationalists, Catholics—as well as a small Jewish congregation—would make Traverse City their home in years to come. Apart from purely religious functions, they bound individuals together in caring for the poor, sick, and elderly, engaging in fundraising activities such as church suppers, and celebrating Holy Days. The cold isolation of winter was made more bearable with social and religious events promoted by the churches and the synagogue.

The church was just one of the civilizing influences desired by early families. Another was the town newspaper. At first sight, Traverse City would seem an unlikely place to publish a newspaper. For one thing, it had few inhabitants: An 1860 census records that only 494 individuals lived in the village. Of them, 204 were "foreign born," many, no doubt, illiterate in English (though native speakers were often illiterate, too). For survival the newspaper would have to sell subscriptions outside Northern Michigan, sending copies through the United States Postal Service.

Not only was readership lacking, commercial support in the form of businesses willing to advertise was similarly absent. The new paper, the *Grand Traverse Herald,* mostly carried advertisements from Detroit businesses, perhaps a favor to the editor, Morgan Bates, who had previous experience editing *The Detroit Advertiser* several years before.

Morgan Bates was a firm abolitionist and his paper reflected his views. Like most newspapers of the era, the *Grand Traverse Herald* was partisan: it was staunchly Republican, supporting Abraham Lincoln with religious fervor. In the first edition of the paper the editor writes:

> In Politics we admit no such word as Neutrality. We hate slavery in all its forms and conditions, and can have no fellowship or compromise with it. We entertain no respect for any party or any religion which sanctions and supports it, we care not from what source they derive their authority; and regard that politician, minister, or layman, who advocates its extension and perpetuity, as an enemy to the Human Race, and false to the God we worship.

Bates was a gifted writer inflamed with a passion for abolition, his enthusiasm often extending beyond that issue to other points in the Republican platform, especially the strong emphasis on morality and temperance. His newspaper—as well as the commitment of the local citizenry to the Union cause—converted the Traverse area into a Republican stronghold for generations to come. It would be 52 years before the local citizenry would turn away from Republicans—and then only to support Progressive Theodore Roosevelt, a former Republican.

Early newspapers were not just about political advocacy; they are also about moral edification, entertainment, and news. The front page of the *Her-*

ald was filled with poems and stories from many sources in the day when copyrights were not respected. One can imagine how settlers would devour such literary offerings in a place devoid of books. Though only a few pages long, the paper was larger than the present-day *Traverse City Record-Eagle*, each page dense with print in the era before photographs were routinely inserted into copy. The inflated prose of the time was not a barrier to the enjoyment of the newspaper.

Newspapers require news. In the middle of the nineteenth century they obtained it by telegraph, letters, and occasionally by reporting. Situated at the end of a long, trackless peninsula, the *Herald* could not catch the drift of national events that circulated along railways and telegraph wires. Indian mail carriers made the trek from Muskegon to Traverse City once a week. In bad wintry weather they sometimes arrived late, making the editor declare ruefully that there would be no new news in that edition. Upon the completion of the railroad in 1873, the Traverse area became connected to the outside world both through regular daily mail delivery and through the telegraph lines that went along the tracks. The news currents flowing from Washington and from Lansing finally washed directly upon the shores of the town.

Civilized societies have libraries. Accordingly, the people of Traverse City began their own library, purchasing volumes using fine money collected by the township. The books were gathered at one business or another, shifting every several years to a new location. The *Herald* occasionally published exhortations to borrowers to return books, those advertisements indicating an organized borrowing system was not in place. Whatever the deficiencies of the public library, its very existence betokened the value settlers placed on learning.

In 1869 the women of Traverse City would create a friendly rival to the Township Library, the Ladies Library. M.E.C. Bates, one of the founding members of the new library, recounted the story of its beginning:

> In our fancy we can see the heated air, see the dusty floor and benches of the almost deserted hall, and I can even remember the droning of a bewildered blue-bottle fly, that had strayed in somehow and doubtless wondered, as he tumbled over the dingy windows, what it was all about, but clearest of all, we can see the little group of women on the front seats, vigorously

Taken about 1869, a view of the Union Street dam on the Boardman River

fanning themselves, and listening to the stirring words of our leader, as, with her flashing black eyes and vivacious manner, she unfolded her plans and wishes to us. Then and there our association sprang, full-fledged, into existence. The records of the society, on the first page of the first volume, say: 'After remarks by various ladies, it was moved that a Ladies' Library Association be organized in Traverse City. Carried unanimously.' It was very simple after all. We merely said: 'Let there be a Ladies Library Association,' and there was a Ladies Library Association.

The women of the Ladies Library Association went to work collecting books, raising money, and planning for a building of their own. With little help from their husbands, they had a great hall constructed near the corner of Cass and Front Streets. The upper floor was to be used as a lecture and entertainment space, while the lower floor housed the library and commercial businesses. Before the opera houses to come, it was the largest meeting place in the village: Susan B. Anthony made an appearance there in her campaign to gain women the right to vote. Later, a more elegant brick building—which still stands—was erected near the corner of Cass and State Streets. It is a monument to the devotion of the pioneer women who took it upon themselves to build a small oasis of civilization in the middle of a vast wilderness.

The story of Traverse City's first school took on the cachet of myth as early historians reported the first teacher, a fifteen-year-old girl named Helen Goodale, leaped from log to log to cross the Boardman, arriving at a log school built in a dense woods. Barely equipped as a proper school with dirt floor and but two windows, it was a primitive building which harbored snakes and—presumably—other kinds of vermin.

The number of children grew rapidly, forcing the district to build and enlarge new buildings, the first of them located near the present Park Place. In 1873 a local census revealed that more than 300 children lived within the district, a milestone allowing school bonds to be sold for the construction of new buildings. A union or high school district could be established when student populations reached that level. Accordingly, a high school was established in 1877, at first in a frame building and later in a brick building located at a place devoted to schooling ever after: the block bounded by Wadsworth and Pine, Seventh and Eighth.

Children went to school to satisfy many purposes of society. Beyond mastering basic literacy and arithmetic, they learned lessons about patriotism, piety, and good manners. The set of readers adopted by the district, the Sander's Readers, taught morality through a variety of tales, reflections, poems, and prayers. In one of them, a child who has been throwing rocks into a pond, watching the waves spread out, is told by his teacher, *And thus, if you keep on learning till you are a man, your mind will become larger and larger, like the waves; and your fame may yet spread all over the world.*

Virtue was not imparted solely by such homilies. School discipline played its role, too. A former student, Thomas T. Bates, remembers his early primary school experience:

> ...the men and women of the Traverse City of to-day who were the little boys and girls of the hamlet in the pine woods of thirty years ago look into the (school) building now as they pass and they can see what the passing stranger or later coming citizen cannot—the little school room with its high silled windows,

and the rows of plain desks and stiff-backed seats on either side and up and down the center, and the teacher's raised platform at the further end with its plain table and never failing, ever restless, switch, and ruler resting thereon.

The switch and the ruler were intended to instill the self-control demanded by career, family life, and participation in the community.

Due to low pay, the insistence that women abandon teaching upon their marriage, and low standards for certification (insuring a large pool of applicants), teachers turned over every year or two; six are listed between the winters from 1851 to 1857. The tenure of students at school was similarly short; after eight grades students would begin their life's work. Only a small minority—largely made up of students from wealthy families—would continue schooling beyond primary school. Those so favored would go on to become doctors, lawyers, college professors, engineers, bankers, and leaders in commerce.

Changes

The earliest photographs of Traverse City show the Boardman River full of logs, the great pine forest south of the river being taken down by loggers, and a busy sawmill and wharf at the edge of the Bay. It did not take long to remove the trees that covered the city-to-be. Pictures taken in the early 1890's show the hills mostly barren except for a beech-maple woods on the southwest hills. Roads were seas of mud in the spring, dusty, rutted paths in the summer, and only suggested places for travel by sleighs in winter.

With the passing of the forest, the sun and wind made the microclimate inhospitable. A wintry wind off the Bay was not mitigated by the trees, nor was the hot wind in August as it swept down the hills to the west. Heavy rains caused floods as the raindrops fell upon sloping ground no longer covered by leaf litter and stabilized by tree roots. By the 1870's Traverse City was a place of dust and mud, sawdust and horse manure, mosquitoes and flies—the incessant noise of construction and destruction replacing the songs of Hermit Thrushes.

If the land was changed, the water was changed even more. The banks of the Boardman River were denuded of trees, the smooth and steep slopes being reserved for rollaways, sites where stacked logs were rolled into the river for transport to the sawmill at its mouth. Ensuing rains would swell the river to great heights, stirring up sediment that carried downstream. Spawning grounds for fish were thereby destroyed, especially those of sturgeon. The damming of the Boardman in 1869 prevented the upstream migration of Great Lakes fish, cutting off the upper reaches of the river to a variety of fish species. All over the Great Lakes, due to habitat destruction and overfishing, catches of white fish, sturgeon, and lake trout plummeted: the commercial catch of whitefish was reduced by nearly a third between 1879 and 1899. Sturgeon disappeared entirely from the Boardman and the arctic grayling, though not definitely a resident of that river, gradually disappeared from nearby river systems such as the Jordan River.

For all the destruction of Nature, by 1880 the goal of planting civilization in Northwestern Lower Michigan was being achieved—but slowly in the eyes of some of its inhabitants. Churches were constructed, students were graduated from high school, books were purchased for libraries, a prosperous newspaper was published on a weekly basis. Missionaries had long since converted most Indians to Christianity. The settlement begun only three decades before had become a village, the county seat with its governmental offices and its court.

Still, people worried about the town's future, for the logging industry would run out of trees soon, closing down sawmills permanently. In response to their concerns, the *Grand Traverse Herald* asked a seventeen-year old lithographer, William Holdsworth, to create a poster advertising Traverse City's advantages to prospective settlers. It was distributed widely in hope of attracting farmers, businessmen, fishermen and hunters, and professionals of all kinds to the area. The *Herald* noted that newspaperman Horace Greely had dismissed northern Michigan as a place of dismal climate, poor soils, and unfriendly swamps. His screed demanded a rebuttal.

Holdsworth's lithograph makes a vivid response to Greely. It shows a view of Traverse City from a point on Old Mission peninsula looking south along West Bay. A boat heads towards the town, its sails billowed with a strong wind astern. Framed by images of trees propping up hunting rifles and fish rods, trees propping up crosscut saws and axes, it tells viewers there are still fish left in the waters, game in the forests, and trees for the cutting. At the bottom are baskets of fruit and produce, a suggestion that farming is likely to be successful. Finally, the traditional romance of Northern Michigan—a view

Holdsworth lithograph (1873) showing Traverse City as seen
from Old Mission Peninsula

of an Indian village—is juxtaposed with modernity—the curve of a railroad track around the Bay. Traverse City has it all.

History is not just about the growth of wealth within a community. It also describes changes in people's outlook on life. The first settlers undertook enormous risks to make their livelihoods here. Many exchanged ordered fields for uncleared land, traded respectable schools for primitive one-room schoolhouses, and swapped clear prospects for earning a living at home for the uncertainty of finding work in an isolated place. They came by foot on Indian trails from southern Michigan and by boat, landing at a barren wharf jutting out from a West Bay beach. One could imagine the dismay they would have felt upon looking at Traverse City for the first time, yet they stayed and raised their families here.

The courage they displayed resonates with us today when we consider the risks they accepted, the harshness of the journey, and the squalor of this small settlement built upon the beach. At the same time, we should consider the fascination and awe they must have felt upon arrival: the beauty of the waters and the towering forests, the howls of wolves at night and the singing of hundreds of birds in day, the busy sounds of the sawmill and the drum song of local Indian bands—and, on the blackest nights, the view of the Milky Way mirrored upon smooth surface of the Bay.

Passenger/freight dock on West Bay, 1908

Becoming a City
1880-1910

The Village: September, 1894

The *Petoskey* let out a cloud of black smoke as it departed the transportation dock, its horn signaling smaller boats to keep away. Clad in long coats in preparation for the voyage to come, passengers waved to friends and family, being careful to hold onto hats in the face of a strong wind from the north. The trip to Chicago would take about twenty-four hours—or so the schedule said—but rough seas could delay their arrival.

The small crowd of well-wishers began the walk back to Front Street, mostly by foot, but a few by bicycle in violation of a prominent sign warning, "No Bicycles." The riders were regarded with silent admiration by some

23

who envied their skill and with disapproval by others who were bothered by the flagrant disrespect of the sign. Still, the walkers spent little time reflecting on the matter as plumes of coal smoke were blowing towards them not only from the *Petoskey* but from the grain carrier *Lineria* nearby and from the *E.A. Johnson* unloading coal at the coal dock. The dock was dirty and loud, offensive to women in particular, with its clatter of machinery, puffing of steam locomotives, shrieks of boat whistles, and occasional light-hearted cursing of sailors and workers.

Although the sky held some light in the west, the sun had set, its rays lingering red upon the horizon, redder than usual because of forest fires burning west and south of the village. The dying light silhouetted the barren hill facetiously named "Mount Ramsdell," in honor of Judge Ramsdell whose home occupied that place. Surrounding hills appeared stark without the trees that had been taken down scarcely a decade ago. West of the Asylum a few great beeches and maples stood upon the hills, reminders to older residents of the forests of their youth.

Its cupolas barely visible in the gathering dusk, the Northern Michigan Asylum showed a few glimmers of light from many windows. It boasted one of Edison's electric generators, providing light to the troubled souls within and to the townspeople who looked at the building from the outside. The city had its own generator, too—a steam powered plant that sent out its own plume of smoke near the dock. Since the construction of the power plant five years before, the night skies of the city burned with the brightness of arc lamps hung from the major street intersections, Front and Union, Front and Cass, and Front and Park Street. The River of Stars disappeared overhead as the electric lamps invaded its domain. City dwellers would have to go to the country to see the meteor showers and the faint stars within Orion and the Big Dipper.

At Front and Union the mighty Hannah and Lay Mercantile building stood mostly dark with but a few windows lighted with incandescent bulbs. The largest department store north of Grand Rapids, it was the pride of the town with its solid three stories occupying half a block. Brick buildings had begun to re-

View of Front Street before 1903

place the frame structures that defined Front Street for the past three decades: the City Opera House across the Street from the Hannah Lay building, the Masonic building next to it, the Beadle building at the corner of Cass and Front, and Steinberg's Opera House between Cass and Park. The community was more than a village, everyone knew: it was a city—and a modern one at that.

Challenges

While logging continued in 1894—the stacks of logs still rolled into the Boardman from the banks of Boardman Lake as well as upstream—it was clear that it could not go on forever. Already small logging towns were disappearing as the trees went down around them—a general store unable to find customers, a blacksmith forced to move on as horse traffic diminished, a school closed for lack of pupils. For a time the founders of Traverse City were worried: after the forests were cleared, how would the city survive?

Lumberman Perry Hannah could not bear to see his town fail. He had put too much of his life into it. In 1873 he had made sure the railroad would not bypass Traverse City by selling bonds to construct a spur from the mainline heading north. As a former legislator, he lobbied Lansing for the construction of a new mental hospital, the Northern Michigan Asylum, at the edge of town. His arguments prevailed and the hospital was completed in 1884, bringing nearly 250 jobs to the community. The building gleamed like a castle, nestled upon the western hills of the city, and residents were proud.

Hannah, himself, was responsible for much economic growth in Traverse City. Realizing the end of logging was at hand, he had the Hannah Lay Company split in two, one branch continuing lumber and real estate operations, and the other dealing with lucrative commercial business. Never one to think small, he established the Hannah and Lay Mercantile Company building at the corner of Union and Front Streets with five bays of show windows displaying everything from cook stoves to the latest fashions. He bought the Park Place Hotel and made it a grand stopping place for visitors. His bank was the largest in the area in terms of capital and size of loans made to local businessmen: he had no problems loaning to potential competitors if the investment advanced the interests of the city.

Before his death in 1904, Perry Hannah could look out from his magnificent home on Sixth Street and survey his kingdom: his flour mill at the Union Street dam to the east, his hotel, the Park Place, to the northeast, his bank, the Traverse City State Bank due north, and even the reminder of his role in securing railroad transportation, railroad tracks not fifty yards from where he lived. It must have been satisfying to see all of those things, while remembering the unmarked wilderness he had explored here more than fifty years before.

Still, the future of the town was not assured. In the second half of the nineteenth century downstate cities grew faster than those of the north. Lansing had a population of 13,102 in 1890, Kalamazoo, 17,853, and Muskegon, 22,702, while the village of Traverse City—soon to be the City of Traverse City—had only 4833 residents, that number rising rapidly to 7,386 four years later. Starting from its humble beginnings as a lumbering town, Traverse City had grown to become the second largest city in the northern Lower Peninsula, after Manistee. That mushroom growth suggested a question: Could the population and the wealth of the community continue to increase in such fashion?

At this time the wealth of the region was largely concentrated in the hands of factory owners and the lumber companies. Workers lived close to the bone, their wages barely covering the costs of food and shelter. In the days before minimum wage standards were established, they survived paycheck to paycheck, hoping injury or illness would not prevent them from going to work. How would they respond to low wages and harsh working conditions? That challenge never goes away; it makes up a common thread that extends throughout all generations.

Responses

In spite of its self-promotion as a resort destination, Traverse City was predominantly an industrial town. Certainly people did come to enjoy the Bay and nearby lakes, occupying resorts and cottages during the summer months, but that seasonal business did not make for a stable economy. Besides, Petoskey had more to offer visitors with its sparkling Bay View development and its attractive summer program of concerts, lectures, and other entertainments. By contrast, Traverse City had dirt under its fingernails and a smudge of smoke in the air it breathed.

The Oval Wood Dish Company was the largest factory in town, spreading out over acres of land at the north end of Boardman Lake near the present public library. It specialized in various hardwood products, manufacturing the majority of clothespins in early twentieth century America. Its namesake product, the oval wood dish, was an not ornamental vessel intended to display fruit, but was a thin-walled container designed to store perishables such as butter, cottage cheese, and meat. It was the Styrofoam tray of its age.

The success of the company was remarkable: by 1912 it was the largest employer in the city with a payroll of 600 workers. Its wages largely determined pay scales for other factories around the area—the Wells-Higman basket company on Boardman Lake, the Potato Implement Company on Front Street, the Traverse City Iron Works on Lake Street, as well as a variety of sawmills at various locations inside and outside the city limits. Given the importance of Oval Wood Dish to the economy of the city, it is worthwhile to look at the wages it paid out to its workers, the work schedule of the day, and the working conditions within the factory.

In 1912 Oval Wood Dish paid its workers a starting wage of one dollar and forty-four cents a day, each workday averaging nine hours. Such a wage seems ridiculously low by today's standards until the value of the dollar is taken into consideration. Allowing for a few paid holidays, beginning workers received about 450 dollars a year, a sum now regarded as poverty wages.

Overhead view of Oval Wood Dish Company

A family of five at that time required about 700 dollars using modern poverty standards. Even with a few dollars earned outside factory work, factory workers' families were often destitute—wages going to pay for necessities rather than going into savings for unemployment, emergencies, or into investments in a home or business.

The Oval Wood Dish Company was hardly alone in paying minimal wages to its workers. In 1891 workers unloading boats at the docks affiliated with the Longshoremen's Association fought wage cutting practices by a local lumber company. They declared that the foreman insisted nonunionized labor could do the work at a fraction of the cost of the unionized crew, convincing barge and ship captains to avoid the union. After angry workers attacked the head of the lumber of company with "something worse than tar and feath-

ers" as he rode on his bicycle, matters came to a head. In the end, however, no promises were made with regard to unionized or nonunionized workers unloading the boats at various ports in the area.

A nine-hour, six-day-a-week work schedule of the Oval Wood Dish Company was a hardship on workers, but for all that, was hardly worse than other factories offered at the time. In 1912 the average workweek for manufacturing plants was 59.3 hours, indicating a six-day, ten-hour schedule. In settling the Oval Wood Dish Company strike, workers accepted a contract that increased hours from nine to ten hours a day, thereby enabling them to earn more. Apparently the increased earnings received was worth it even if they had to stay at the factory an extra hour every day to get it.

Working conditions at Oval Wood Dish most likely resembled those at other factories throughout the United States: dangerous machinery, air pollution in the form of particulates and harmful chemical substances, inadequate training for new hires, absence of clearly defined procedures to be followed in case of emergencies, prompt medical treatment in case of accidents, and more. The plant suffered a major fire in 1896, hardly an unusual occurrence among sawmills and factories at a time when coal and wood fired steam engines provided power for saws, lathes, routers, and other woodworking machinery.

The Oval Wood Dish Company supported injured workers, paying salaries up to six months for accidents suffered on the job. Such benevolence may have been generous when compared to other such plants, but payouts were often insufficient to cover lifetime expenses for severely injured workers. In the absence of contracts clearly spelling out terms of employment, charity depends upon the good will of the company, not the obligations set out in agreements signed by workers and management.

Who were the workers that toiled in Traverse City factories at the turn of the century? First, many were women. The Oval Wood Dish Company hired many of them because they could do the job for less money. When the company settled the 1912 strike by increasing the length of the workday, it was compelled to pay women workers more as a stipulation of the agreement. In the early twentieth century women workers would strike or threaten to strike in many local industries: telephone operators, candy makers at the Straub Brothers and Amiotte company on Front and Hall Street, and cigar manufacturers. Labor militancy was hardly confined to men.

Second, workers were frequently immigrants, many with Bohemian roots. They worked for low wages to support their families, living precariously from paycheck to paycheck. The Straub Brothers and Amiotte Candy Company hired many of them, especially women. In a story published just after the First World War, the *Traverse City Record-Eagle* told how a female worker at the plant had heard her boss casually refer to his workers as "Bohunks," a term that fuses "Bohemian" with "Hunky," the second word a pejorative aimed at workers of European descent. The woman had to recant her accusation in the face of attacks by the press and management, but in her remark she revealed the makeup of the workforce as well as prejudice levied towards it.

Third, the workforce of Traverse City was not unionized, a fact common in towns without highly profitable manufacturing plants such as machine shops. Sawmills, companies specializing in oval wood dishes and clothespins, candy factories, and small enterprises devoted to making cigars did not pay good wages, when compared to factories employing skilled labor. In the absence of unions, labor stood at a disadvantage when it came to workers receiving a fair share of profits.

At the height of Traverse City's growth, there were other ways to make a living besides factory work. F.E. Walker's *Traverse City Directory of 1894* lists no fewer than 119 contractors, builders, and carpenters, 29 masons, and 33 painters. Construction was booming as residences, businesses, and factories were built at a pace never to be duplicated. Most were private contractors, working for themselves and employing family members or a few hired hands. As long as times were good, there was good money to be made.

Farmers had as much trouble making a living as factory workers. Some received land grants as a result of their service in the Civil War. They cleared the forest and removed the stumps, erected house and barn, and stretched fences around pastures, becoming fairly well-off in comparison to factory workers. Many others did not own their farms, only working them for an absentee owner or hiring themselves out at harvest time to make a few dollars. The seasonal nature of farming was especially hard on them as there was no money to be earned in winter. Money could be made in farming if the land was good, if prices were high, and if the farmer owned the property. Of course, as it has always been, a seasonal drought or flood could wipe out a farmer in a single year.

From the beginning of the Traverse settlement, observers noted that the area was perfectly suited for growing fruit. An early editor of the *Grand Traverse Herald*, M.L. Leach, predicted the Traverse region would export fruit of all kinds—apples, plums, apricots, and cherries. He was right: within his lifetime schooners laden with barrels of apples would set off for the Chicago market. Plums, apricots, and cherries would follow.

One steady source of jobs and wealth was the Northern Michigan Asylum, later to be named the Traverse City State Hospital. Work was not seasonal and paid a moderate, if not excessive wage. In addition, workers did not have to endure layoffs as longshoremen, farmers, and sawmill workers did. The Asylum offered jobs like those of college towns: reliable work at reasonable pay. For nearly a hundred years after its founding the hospital enhanced the stability of the town's economy. In 1894 it employed 250 persons serving nearly 1000 patients. Like other cities with state institutions, Traverse City could grow using funds collected from the State of Michigan. A boon to the economy in diverse ways, this influx of money enabled local business to supply goods to the hospital and indirectly encouraged the hotel trade as visitors to the Asylum often required overnight stays.

James Decker Munson, the first superintendent of the Asylum (his tenure: 1884-1923), did not regard his institution as a vehicle for bringing prosperity to a remote city, but as a hospital for the mentally ill. He rejoiced in taking patients out of shamefully kept attics and basements, out of inadequate county poorhouses, out of jails and placing them in large state-run institutions like his own. He advocated adequate training of asylum attendants, even starting a nursing school of his own. Although effective treatments for a variety of illnesses were years in the future, patients were generally cared for decently. With many patient windows facing a gorgeous arboretum, the hospital displayed a value commonly expressed during the nineteenth century: Nature heals. True or not, that belief did nothing to hurt patients—and certainly made their lives more pleasant.

The values that shaped the community carried over from those of the previous generation. Besides an intense drive to present a modern face to the world, Traverse City wished to declare it was also civilized. With Perry Hannah donating land across from his home on Sixth Street, the city secured 20,000 dollars from Andrew Carnegie to build a new public library. Its classical presentation with pillars at its entrance, a pediment with sculpture relief, and a rotunda facing the river reminded visitors of larger such buildings in Southern Michigan. Built in 1892 the City Opera House offered a splendid venue for plays, concerts, and high school activities. A block east on Front Street, Steinberg's Opera House presented similar fare. Few towns the size of Traverse City could boast one large theater, let alone two.

Townspeople took pride in their schools. In the late nineteenth and early twentieth centuries high schools mostly prepared students for college. In an era before industrial, commercial, and agricultural education, they offered a curriculum emphasizing Latin, Greek, literature, and higher mathematics to students often favored by family background and wealth. Traverse City mostly followed this model, though it instituted a commercial program as early as 1886, a course of study designed for students who wished to go into business.

With a student body selected from families devoted to education—and able to keep their children out of the workforce until graduation—standards were high. Examinations for the previous week's material were held on Mondays, the standard for passing set at 80 percent. Students could choose among three courses of study—English, Latin, or Scientific—depending upon their interests and future plans for college. However, high school graduation could prepare some students for work immediately: teaching. At a time when standards for teaching were low, it was possible to obtain lower level certification by graduation from the high school.

The high school attracted students from rural areas outside the district. Tuition was inexpensive: ten cents per week for high school students, and 25 to 30 cents for students at lower levels. The superintendent assured families that good room and board could be obtained for as little as 2.50 to 3.00 per week. To earn extra money many families living close to the school were eager to take in students from other districts.

The first Catholic school in Traverse City was built on Union Street between Seventh and Eighth. Father Ziegler of Traverse City successfully applied to the Sisters of St. Dominic of New York to recruit staff for the new school. Upon their arrival, a school (and convent) was rapidly constructed, opening in 1877. Sixteen years later a magnificent new building was completed, accommodating 150 students at the Cass Street location of the present St. Francis High School. Serving an ethnically diverse population including French, Bohemian, Polish, and Irish immigrants, the Catholic school system has deep roots in the early history of the city.

Traverse City was an exciting place to live in 1890's. People occupied themselves mostly with the business of making a living, but they did find time for recreation, participation in cultural activities, and school and church affairs. More well-to-do residents enjoyed swimming at the Wequetong, a social club located near the mouth of the Boardman River that featured swimming and tennis in summer as well as a variety of other entertainments. The Bay, nearby lakes, and the river offered opportunities for swimming, fishing, and boating to everyone, though environmental degradation of the water kept sensible people away from the most polluted areas.

People were joiners of clubs and benevolent societies. Thirty-nine of them are listed in *Walker's Traverse City Directory of 1894*. Their focus was wide-ranging, including a veterans group (the Grand Army of the Republic), agricultural societies like the Grange, groups with cultural goals such as the Ladies Library, traditional fraternal organizations like the Masons, and organizations focusing on social change such as the Women's Christian Temperance Union. For active or passive recreation, the town boasted three baseball clubs: the Traverse City Baseball Club, the Red Star Baseball Club, and the Asylum Baseball Club. The Pirouette Club enjoyed dancing and the Shakespeare Club presumably enjoyed putting on plays. At this time bicycles and roller skates were immensely popular among old and young alike. Among entertainments coming to the area from elsewhere, circuses and traveling shows provided townspeople with glimpses of the outside world. Ringling Brothers Circus and Buffalo Bill's Wild West Circus both visited Traverse City in the closing years of the nineteenth century.

Still, opportunities for leisure were hard to come by in an era when workers put in ten-hour days six days a week. Besides the impoverished working class, the truly destitute were too busily engaged in mere survival to enjoy leisure and cultural assets like the City Opera House. Grouped with the insane and criminals, they came to poverty because of their "moral failure" in the language of the day. In short, they deserved their station in life because of intemperance, indolence, and bad judgment. The notion that society should play a role in uplifting them had not taken root in the consciousness of most citizens.

The condition of local Indians was especially dire. An 1889 article in the *Detroit News* described the Indian settlement Peshabestown in Leelanau County:

> Struggling along the west shore of Grand Traverse Bay, for a mile or more, is a double line of houses in all stages of decay. There is the house that is a total wreck, with skeleton rafters from which the shingles and roof boards were blown years ago, while an occasional rust eaten and decrepit nail holds a side board to the precarious upright pieces, showing dilapidation of the incipient, progressive and "got there" kind. Interspersed between these ghosts of dwellings is an occasional house in good repair, in front of which may frequently be seen a squaw wielding an ax and making the chips fly like a real man. If her husband has succeeded in [bringing] a few logs to the front door, he leaves her to manufacture it into fuel. Around the mother may be seen a stepladder like array of tawny urchins, regardless alike of the present careless of the future…

The article goes on to say that twenty-five years earlier the community appeared to be prosperous, but had since fallen on hard times. The priest of the local church, Father Ignatius Mrak, was forthright about where to cast blame for the current sad condition of his flock:

> Once every Indian had land, and you see the houses they built. You also see the decay, and the explanation is simple— white man and whisky. The white men have made them drunk and robbed them of their lands, and now they seem to work

Railroad crossing Boardman River at its mouth

only to get money to buy the accursed drink. Often I have to go to Traverse City and other places where my people have been to work, to see that the poor deluded children get their pay and do not spend it for drink. It is hard to Christianize an Indian when he sees white men, whom he supposes to be Christians, robbing him and his brethren.

Whatever the magnificence of Traverse City's Opera Houses, libraries, and schools, a large population of Indians, poor farmers, and factory laborers never entered them: they hardly knew they were there. Instead of those cultural and entertainment venues, they frequented saloons and billiard parlors on Front Street east of Park. Well separated from the Hannah Lay Mercantile Company, eleven of them crowded a two block area. It was the seamy side of town—everybody knew it—and young people were enjoined to keep away. In fact, one selling point of the new library (1904) on Sixth Street was that it would keep students away from such bad influences.

Changes

The oldest settlers must have regarded the Traverse City of the 1890's with mixed feelings. Formerly a gorgeous pine forest, it was now a barren plain. Where the river, upstream from its mouth, used to run cold and clear, now it was filled with the residue of sawmills, sediment, and human-generated debris and waste. The old beach on West Bay spoke of gulls, sand, dune grass, the reflection of sky, and the lapping of waves, while the new one was about the soot of railroads, blasts from the horns of steamers, the smell of horse manure and coal-fired steam engines, and the products of the sawmill scattered haphazardly between the waterfront and Front Street. The passage between the two worlds had been gradual, accelerating over the past two decades. The loss of Nature was painful to some, but to others it was only attendant to progress.

Yet Perry Hannah, the individual largely responsible for the ravaging of the environment, chose to build his retirement home on Sixth Street within fifty yards of a railroad track, the shrieks of the locomotive and its sooty defilement of snow an accepted cost of civilization. The economic advancement of citizens, the construction of a new library, the grand school built a block from his home, the churches, the vibrant newspapers (there were three of them at Hannah's death)—all of these things easily paid for the barrenness of the land and the degradation of the river and bayshore. The sacrifice was worth it.

Still, there were those who lamented what was lost. F.E. Walker in his *Directory*, speaking as an architect and planner, spells out the defects of the city:

> ...it needs a city park, a good large one, one owned by the city and supported at city expense. It should be on the bay shore: it should be laid out with numerous walks and drives with the portions between well seeded down and set out to shade trees, and plenty of rustic seats should be provided for the public; it should be well supplied with water, either artesian or city, and it might not be out of place to have fountain in the center of it. It also seems as if it would be a profitable investment for some one to erect a bathing house on the bay shore and keep suits to rent at a nominal price, that visitors and residents might avail themselves of an invigorating bath in Lake Michigan. With these

features alone added, Traverse City might be made a popular summer resort of itself. Without these it is out of the race and tourists must go farther north.

In the last sentence Walker hints of the attractions of Charlevoix, Petoskey, and Harbor Springs. In contrast to those places the city was only a rude industrial town.

Beyond the unsightliness of its industrial waterfront, the city faced genuine threats to public safety and health. A four-inch rain on August 22, 1898 brought home to residents what indiscriminate logging and inattention to soil conservation can do. A flood on Kid's Creek (then called Mill Creek) swept away bridges, trees, wooden sidewalks, coops of chickens, and electric light poles. Trapped within their narrow stables, terrified horses had to be freed from the rushing water. One family escaped from its home by rowboat, leaving by way of a second story window.

The devastation of the flood was caused by the removal of vegetation near the creek and on the slopes on the west side of town. Without a network of roots to anchor the soil, the rain drove the creek beyond its banks, creating at one point, a raging river fifty feet wide that crossed Division Street. Trees, residents learned, served a function besides adding grace and beauty to the city landscape. They could prevent an environmental catastrophe.

The neglect of the environment could produce disease, too. In 1906 thirty-five city residents came down with typhoid, a figure probably far smaller than the actual number, given inadequate reporting of the day. Rapidly word went out across the state that Traverse City was suffering an epidemic of the disease—an insult to the town in an age that already realized typhoid was

Flood on Mill Creek (Kids Creek), 1898. Houses are on Fifth Street.

spread by bad water. The city obtained its water at the time from an intake that extended a short distance into West Bay so close to shore that contamination from human and animal waste was nearly certain. It would take many years until the problem was fixed.

For all its pride in its new brick buildings—the new Asylum, the Hannah and Lay Mercantile building, two Opera Houses, the Beadle Building at the corner of Cass and Front—the city mainly consisted of frame buildings perched upon a sand plain. They were built along treeless streets on roads made dusty in drought and muddy in rain. The snow came as a benediction, covering up the abused ground around the houses, though soot from coal and wood fires discolored it rapidly. The city was not beautiful.

Nor was the river. It was widely regarded as a system of removing waste from the city's homes, businesses, and factories. Sewage pipes emptied directly into the river, receiving no treatment at all. At a time before the germ theory of disease had penetrated public decision-making, officials believed that disease agents could be diluted by sending contaminated water deeper into the Bay. Of course, germs are not gotten rid of so easily: they lurk in the water mixing with it, eventually finding the intake to the water works, thereby spreading disease.

At the turn of the twentieth century people took joy in the advances of technology: electricity and electric lights, the bicycle, telephone and telegraph, photography, and gas heating. Traverse City residents believed their town was at the forefront of modernism In fact, compared to other regions of the United States, some technologies—like the telephone—advanced slowly, while others—like electricity—were adopted rapidly and with great enthusiasm.

Though Alexander Graham Bell invented the telephone in 1876, telephones did not spread rapidly across the United States for reasons of high cost to consumers, the inhibiting nature of patent rights, and the difficulty in extending telephone lines among residences, businesses, and factories. By 1893 only .4 percent of Americans had telephone service, a startlingly low figure for such a useful invention. At this time, mostly drawn from a population of wealthy residents and businesses, Traverse City only had 77 telephone users, a figure that translates into .01 percent of the village population. Whatever the cause—cost, marketing, or difficulty in stringing lines—Traverse City residents did not buy into the new technology.

Electricity was different. Wabash, Indiana was the first town to light its downtown with towers of arc lights in 1879 with Detroit and Chicago quickly following with their own lighting systems. Traverse City got into the game with a steam-powered plant located near the foot of Union Street on the Bay in 1889. The effect of incandescent lighting on townspeople must have been overwhelming in view of the fact they had lived their lives under the weak illumination of kerosene lamps, candles, and the fires in their fireplaces. It is said that the arc lights placed at major city intersections were so bright that people could see colors of the clothes people were wearing even on moonless nights.

The Colombian Exposition, held in 1893, only heightened people's infatuation with Edison's incandescent light bulbs. Five thousand arc lights and 90,000 incandescent bulbs converted Chicago into a "White City" with the dazzling display. To behold the miracle of light Traverse City residents could travel to the Exposition easily by steamship or by railroad. Upon their return they demanded the same miracle in their hometown.

Henry D. Campbell's steam powered electric plant was hardly adequate to meet the demand for power. In 1894 a new company, Boardman River Light and Power, built a hydroelectric dam three miles south on the Boardman River, afterwards building another facility downstream (Sabin dam). Shortly thereafter, a new company, Queen City Light and Power, constructed the Keystone and Brown Bridge dams. When the City purchased Queen City, a foundation for a publicly owned utility was laid, Traverse City Light and Power.

Bicycles were the rage during the late nineteenth and early twentieth centuries, not just for recreation, but for transportation. Before the automobile had made its entrance, residents—both men and women—peddled to work and went for "joy rides" on weekends. The 1900 Polk Directory listed six sources for bike sales and three repair shops. The *Jail Record of Grand Traverse County* records no fewer than 26 arrests for violation of the bicycle ordinance in town, a number far exceeding those for larceny (7) and for assault and battery (4). Apparently riders rode on certain sidewalks at the wrong time, rode faster than six miles per hour, or failed to sound a bell or gong upon approaching a pedestrian. The willingness to prosecute bicycle offenders foreshadowed the avalanche of traffic tickets to come with the arrival of the automobile.

Enthusiasm for anything deemed "modern" was a value especially cherished at the turn of the century—and with good reason. Older citizens could remember the time before flush toilets, electric lights, telephones, gas heat, and bicycles—and did not want to go back, while the young embraced technology for its novelty and fun. The Women's Club featured programs about electricity and modern hygiene in the home and the High School supported a club called the Students Scientific Association. The lionization of figures like Thomas Edison and Alexander Graham Bell in school textbooks further demonstrated the hold technology held over the young. In their eyes the twentieth century to come would be full of all sorts of wonderful things. How right they were!

But the values of the past were hardly neglected by people of the 1890's. Patriotism flowered with the victories of the United States during the Spanish American War, stimulating parades and patriotic outbursts on the Fourth of July. Townspeople celebrated the Fourth with footraces, stilt races, sack races, and horse races. They cheered as the Hannah Rifles, Perry Hannah's own militia, freshly returned from Cuba after the war, marched past in uniform. They conducted parades and baseball games—once inviting a female daredevil, Miss Mabel Belmont, to parachute from a smoke-filled balloon—while riding a bicycle—as the grand finale for the day's celebration. She landed safely, though with a slight bruise, since weather conditions did not permit her balloon to reach the required height.

Traverse City celebrated its own place in Northern Michigan by constructing a magnificent county courthouse building in 1900. It was built upon a raised platform of earth beside the Boardman River, its elevation signifying the supremacy of the law and justice in governing all human disputes. A wide expanse of lawn facing Boardman Avenue made it possible for notable persons to give speeches in front of an audience of interested townspeople. The courthouse was not just a place where justice was meted out, but also a place where civil discourse could take place.

In examining the values of the nineteenth century, none was more important than personal morality. James Decker Munson tells a contemporary audience how mental illness can be avoided:

> Children should be taught the necessity of obedience and truthfulness, and above, all, the necessity for self-control; and as they grow in years and in intelligence they should be admonished about certain vicious practices and taught the dangers which attend the abuse of alcoholics and narcotics.

In other words a failure in moral teaching can bring about insanity. Similarly, men become criminals because they failed to learn the moral lessons of their youth. Arthur McDonald, a writer of the time, expresses it this way:

The delinquent [criminal] classes approximate nearest to the normal type [class], for the majority deviate principally in one respect, that is, in a weakness of moral sense that gives away [sic] to temptation.

McDonald expresses the prevailing view of his time that, for the most part, poverty grew out of immorality. Certainly some persons had no money for legitimate reasons: accident, death of a spouse, illness, or unemployment. For those people society made some small provision. The Boardman Valley Hospital, founded in 1911, took in a few of them—women without support, some "feebleminded" who had trouble keeping jobs, homeless elderly persons—but it was hardly big enough to serve the needs of the community. Traverse City had its own "Poor Fund," a budget category that existed between 1898 and 1904. It made grants for food, burials, medical treatment, and housing, but, again, was hardly sufficient to help all those in need. The social safety net of the nineteenth century was a torn and ragged affair dropping those without support of family—the handicapped, injured, sick, elderly, and young—into lives of hunger, homelessness, and joblessness.

From the perspective of decision-makers of the time, most of the poor were not blameless; they drank too much, they refused to work, or they made bad decisions. They deserved the terrible lives they lived and society was not to blame. Only after the suffering of the Great Depression would Traverse City—and the nation—decide that judgment was too harsh, that society had to play a role in providing jobs and support for those less fortunate.

Despite large numbers of people living shattered lives, residents of the city were optimistic about the future. The coming century would see wonders more grand than the telephone and the electric light. They imagined machines would lighten the workload, new medicines would cure disease, and a wealthier world would bring about universal peace. They were, of course, both right and wrong. The twentieth century did, indeed, deliver on many of its promises: the automobile made short trips easy, the airplane made long trips short. Medicine did conquer tuberculosis, one of the main killers of the previous century. But world peace did not come, the quarrelsome nature of human beings asserting itself no matter the stunning advance of technology.

The dedication of Clinch Park

CHAPTER THREE

Economic Collapse
1910-1940

Traverse City: September, 1919

A south wind blew gently from the city towards the wharf carrying the fumes of the gas plant, the smoke of a switching engine pushing a line of flatcars loaded with lumber, and the odor of horse manure that pervaded the air of the city after the rain. In addition there was a new smell: the exhaust of automobiles. They came in all sizes, mostly black, often polished bright by their proud owners. Whether doing errands or joy riding, drivers shared the streets with horses, bicycles, pedestrians, and occasional scavengers ranging from gulls to rats. They drove fast by the standards of the time, often as fast as 25 miles per hour, a speed deemed excessive by city officials. Neither bicyclists nor pedestrians were ready to give way to the four-wheeled competitors for right-of-way and accidents were common. Without standard highway signs pointing to dangerous intersections, sharp curves ahead, and pedestrian crossways, traffic knew no rules.

Steamers stood at the dock, the mighty *Illinois* and the *Missouri*, among others, offering transportation to ports along Lake Michigan all the way to Chicago. The Traverse Bay Line with its smaller boat, the *Columbia*, had gone bankrupt only a few years before, cutting off connections to Suttons Bay, Northport, Elk Rapids, and Norwood. Travelers would have to use rail service, instead.

The Ott Sawmill stood between the Boardman River and West Bay, the products of its activity lying roundabout: stacks of lumber, piles of sawdust, discarded slabs of wood, and neatly piled logs awaiting the saws. Dirty sand and railroad cinders provided the foundation upon which the mill sat with a few trees providing rare respite from the sun in summer. In winter snow made sooty from steam locomotives lay all around.

The Boardman River, too, suffered from the consequences of industry and commerce. It moved a load of rubbish, sawmill cast-offs, and human waste into the West Arm of Grand Traverse Bay. Fish taken from the river were eaten at the fisherman's peril—better to fish on an inland lake away from town or upon the Bay well north of the city. Children were warned not to play in the river, especially where the sewage pipes emptied into the flow as it came out of Union Street dam. It was not safe.

Traverse City itself looked well enough. Illuminated at night, it presented a fair appearance to the farmers who ventured into town from their kerosene lamp-lit homes. The Lyric movie theater changed shows practically every night and people could not get enough of them. The opera houses were still grand, both Steinberg's and the City Opera House, presenting plays, lectures, and concerts. More interesting than those entertainments were the people that attended them.

The age of style had arrived: It was the threshold of the twenties. Fashionable young women stepped out of cars in dresses cut well above the ankle, with lowered neck lines—and they had begun to bob their hair. Hats were big, not yet assuming the contour of the head that close-fitting cloches would display later in the next decade. And the men? Fashionable to be sure, but it was not their turn to shine.

Challenges

Beginning before the First World War, the industrial economy of Traverse City cooled from the high-pitched fervor it experienced at the turn of the century. The Oval Wood Dish Company, the city's largest employer, left town to start operations in Tupper Lake, New York. The city's population dropped from 12,115 in 1915 to 10,925 in 1920. At the same time Grand Traverse County shrank from a population of 23,784 in 1910 to 19,518 in 1920, showing a regional loss of residents. In 1919 fifty of the state's 83 counties were ranked ahead of Grand Traverse County in the value of taxable property: Muskegon had nearly three times as much, Saginaw more than five times. Seeking better livelihoods, workers spilled out of Northern Michigan like water from an open faucet.

The Polk Directory tells how construction vanished in the years after the boom. Where the 1894 F.E. Walker Directory listed 119 carpenters, contractors, and builders, the 1919-20 Polk has only nineteen. Instead of 29 masons, only two appear at the later time. Among manufacturing firms, ten cigar makers were reduced to five. A bright possibility for the town flamed out as the Napolean Automobile Company failed after only two years of business in the 1920's.

While the rest of Michigan was undergoing rapid growth, the Traverse area was caught in an economic vortex consisting of unprofitable companies connected to the lumber industry, a seasonal resort business that could not compete with Petoskey and Charlevoix, and an agricultural base that could not pay decent wages to farm workers and processors. By contrast, Southeastern Michigan had hitched its wagon to the rising star of the automobile industry, its increased tax revenues paying for city improvements such as parks, museums, and libraries.

Besides industry, agriculture was in trouble, too. All across Michigan—and especially in Northern Michigan—farmers left the land, often abandoning their rural dwellings to find jobs in the city. The total number of Michigan farms declined from a peak of 206 thousand in 1910 to only 53 thousand in 1993, much of that drop occurring in the twenties and thirties. Unsurprisingly, farmland rapidly declined in value, the value dropping from 75 dollars per acre in 1920 to 45 fifteen years later. Abandoned homesteads dot the forest landscape in Grand Traverse and Leelanau counties, their presence marked by a caved-in root cellar, a dump, and omnipresent lilacs fighting for survival as larger trees take over. A 1912 postcard sent by an emigrant to Detroit tells the story:

> Hello Jack: How is everybody in Leland? Heard Tiny is going back to Detroit again. You better come down, too. Lots of work... Bill

If it were to survive and prosper, Traverse City would have to reinvent itself. It could continue to attract small businesses by virtue of its low labor costs and its absence of a unionized labor force. It could attract visitors with new resorts and hotels, providing them with things to do and places to go. It could develop the fruit industry, building more facilities for processing apples, pears, plums, apricots, peaches, and cherries. In fact, the city tried all of these things—with varying success—but the momentum propelling the state towards wealth did not seem to touch Northern Michigan. Saginaw, Flint, Grand Rapids—and above all, Detroit—prospered as the north shrank.

The sunny optimism of the nineteenth century gave way to anxiety in the twentieth. Could Traverse City—which began so auspiciously—discover a way to preserve itself in the face of change coming from all sides: technological changes like the automobile and social changes like the new-fangled movies of the twenties? This was the question city leaders would have to answer.

Responses

1919 was a tumultuous year for labor relations across the United States. That year one out of five workers nation-wide was involved in some sort of work action. The situation in Traverse City was no different. Wells-Higman fruit basket makers, women workers at the Johnson Cigar Company, and

Potato Implement Company employees all went on strike that year, while workers at Straub Brothers and Amiotte Candy Company were on the verge of a labor action. In 1912 and 1917 the Oval Wood Dish Company suffered one-day strikes, those walkouts perhaps partly hastening the company's departure from the city. Since Oval Wood Dish was the main employer in town at the time, wage settlements there would influence working conditions and wages elsewhere.

There were richer companies that were hiring downstate, especially those connected to the auto industry. The words of a striking worker at the Wells-Higman plant explained labor's position with regard to wages and the competition with downstate factories:

> The situation has arrived at a point where either we must get an increase in the wage scale, or go to some of the southern Michigan cities or cities throughout the east, where we can make more money. If we choose the latter course, our families will remain here, for Traverse City is the best place in the world to live. I asked most of the men of their decision in the matter last night and this morning, and so far I have found not one who intends to go back on the job at the present wage scale.

The town's very survival was at stake. The worker's statement, "Traverse City is the best place in the world," no doubt kept some on the job, as they sacrificed their economic security for the natural beauty of the area. At this time, the saying became popular: "A view of the Bay is worth half the pay."

One solution to the city's dilemma lay in attracting more visitors to the area. Traverse City was far outshone in this regard by Charlevoix, Petoskey, Harbor Springs, and other communities along the shores of Lakes Huron and Michigan. Bay View, a Methodist cottage community near Petoskey, offered concerts, lectures, classes, and recreational activities for summer visitors both inside and outside the encampment. Harbor Springs and Charlevoix attracted many summer residents from Chicago, offering them respite from the savage heat of their city.

By contrast, Traverse City had little to offer. A resort named "Edgewood" lay at the base of Old Mission Peninsula, a modest development by any standard. The Baptist resort occupied land in Leelanau county only a few miles from town, but it hardly could compete with Petoskey's Bay View. In town, the

Front Street, early twenties

beaches on West Bay were fouled with debris, sewage, and floating residues of both steam locomotives and steam boats. Many knowledgeable town residents kept away from the bay—at least where the Boardman River unloaded its effluent into the water. It was a wise decision since it was common knowledge that typhoid was carried in dirty water, that Traverse City had experienced an epidemic of the disease in 1906.

Understanding that Traverse City could not compete with profitable industries downstate, town leaders resolved to play upon the area's strengths—chiefly its natural beauty. They had to plant trees along paved streets and walkways. They had to clean up filth and debris in the Boardman River. They had to make the waterfront into a gorgeous park, replacing the ugliness of a sawmill, the railroads, and industrial boat docks with trees, grass, a bath house, and benches to sit on. They had to do something about the rats that plagued the city. They had to pull out ragweed that made summer visitors sneeze from the pollen. It was a monumental task they had put before themselves.

In the late nineteenth century the City Beautiful Movement had spread across the nation. People were tired of the railroads running through the center of town, the smoke from factories, barren concrete vistas, the dust and mud of unpaved streets, and crowded, unbroken lines of workers homes along roadways. Soldiers returning from World War I remembered the broad avenues of Paris with its trees, parks, and fountains and longed to bring that vision to their hometowns. While beginning its effort later than large cities like Chicago and Detroit, Traverse City was not immune to the City Beautiful Movement: it began to remake itself.

To begin with, the city began to pave many residential streets, installing curb-and-gutter, laying in sidewalks, and planting trees between the streets and the walkways. But—most important—it began to take back the beach from industrial interests, creating Clinch Park in 1931.

At the beginning of the Great Depression residents were unwilling to pass a bond to finance construction of the new park. Instead, city leaders organized a effort that enlisted the labor, skills, talent, and equipment of the entire community. The *Traverse City Record-Eagle* reported that 500 workers were expected to participate, every local business supplying at least one of them. Thirty-seven small trucks, two tractors, two steam cranes, and a flotilla of 12 boats assembled on a single day in October to remove debris, mud, stones, and concrete slabs. Laborers built a barrier against the waves and graded the higher ground, seeding it with grass and other plantings. The Women's Club supplied 42 pans of beans to feed the workers, prepared in 42 separate kitchens. At the end of the day the newspaper approvingly noted how many unemployed men participated in the building of the new Clinch Park. Rich and poor, citizens had come together to make something magnificent.

The Boardman River was another front in the battle to clean the city. From Boardman Lake to its mouth at the Bay, it was filthy, untreated sewage entering the water from numerous points along its path. Bond issues financing a new sewage treatment plant failed three times, opposition centering on its necessity, its effectiveness, its cost, and the means by which it would be funded and maintained. In the end, the state of Michigan compelled the city to cease and desist the pollution of the Boardman River. A plan was settled upon in 1931 and voters finally passed the bond proposal that allowed construction to begin. At last, after years of logging abuse, sewage disposal, and industrial contamination, the river would begin its long journey towards restoration.

Still, there was much to be done. In 1924 the city resolved to rid the town of rats, bringing in an outsider, Helen Caldwell, to run the campaign. Her pleas urging residents to buy rat poison made a small dent in the rat population. Children rewarded with ten cents for every rat tail reduced it further—

at least temporarily. Weekly pickup of trash no doubt had a greater effect as it removed food sources for the animal. Most important of all was educating the human population about destroying rat homes and keeping all kinds of food away from them.

With the best of intentions, the city was bent on ridding streets and neighborhoods of vermin and pests of every kind. The Rod and Gun Club shot crows; young marksmen were encouraged to shoot sparrows; farmers and city residents alike used arsenic to poison grasshoppers. Offensive plants were not immune to the assaults of the citizenry. Kids who picked sufficient amounts of ragweed were rewarded with money or movie tickets. Poplar trees were taken down because of their penchant for sending roots into sewer lines. Throughout the middle of the twentieth century the battle to civilize this small town in Northern Michigan was waged by methods both ridiculous and sensible. In the end, the battle against rats was quite successful, while those against sparrows, grasshoppers, ragweed, and poplars were abandoned as human combatants lost interest in the fighting.

In the middle of the Great Depression, the city accomplished small cleanup jobs without spending taxpayer money. In 1934 it issued scrip, local money which it used to pay workers to remove debris from the Boardman River below the Union Street dam. A hundred businesses—ranging from grocery stores to Milliken's department store—agreed to accept the currency in lieu of hard-to-get United States dollars. With every transaction a special stamp was affixed to the back of the scrip, one stamp put on weekly or else it could not be redeemed for a real dollar at the end of a year. That way, money would be circulated among merchants, not just hoarded. In general the local currency experiment was regarded as a success, though merchants were glad to abandon money that required them to keep track of stamps.

The rise of the automobile brought about a sea change to the Traverse City community. For one thing, it hastened the end of steamship and railroad passenger service to the city. The Michigan Transit Company stopped boat service to Chicago in 1930. The railroads continued for three more decades with service continually reduced as automobiles and buses provided transportation both cheaper and more convenient for the majority of visitors.

Auto transportation required more than reliable four-wheeled motor machines: it required good roads. Early roads were little more than places where vehicles and horses traveled. Composed of clay, sand, and pebbles—

graded or not—they had no graveled shoulders with trees planted at the very edges, this practice increasing the likelihood of smashups. In the dry days of summer, open-air occupants were covered with dust; in the rainy days of spring they suffered insults of mud. Something had to be done about roads if they were to become avenues for the tourist trade.

Respected businessman Frank Hamilton of Traverse City took on the challenge of remaking the road system of Northern Michigan. Realizing summer visitors would need a smooth, straight highway from Chicago and the South, he championed the Dixie Highway, a route between Mackinaw City and southern Florida. The highway would have two branches in Michigan: an eastern route through Detroit and Southeastern Michigan and a western route hugging the shore of Lake Michigan. It would be paved, for the most part, or at least made of macadam, a pavement composed of crushed stone that locks together tightly. It would be wide enough to accommodate two vehicles side-by-side and would be graded with a central crown. On such a road travelers could enjoy speeds of twenty-five or thirty miles per hour at least. No longer would summer visitors have to depend on train schedules; now they could leave whenever they wished.

The Dixie Highway became a reality. By 1915 it extended north and south for 1700 miles, carrying northerners to the south over the cold winter months and southerners to the cool north in the summer. Within Michigan much of it overlapped with the Michigan Pike, a named road for in-state tourist travel. The Dixie Highway, though long gone from our consciousness, still continues in the road names of Southeastern Michigan. Along the western shore of Lake Michigan a small section of road north of Torch Lake bears the name to this day.

A monument stands to commemorate auto-tourism near the village of Kewadin. Dedicated to Hugh J. Gray, the "Dean of American Tourism" according to the affixed bronze plaque, it was constructed in 1937 before its namesake's death. Gray promoted tourism through establishing Michigan tourist offices in cities like Chicago and Cincinnati, advertising boldly in all media, supporting summer festivals like the Cherry Festival in Traverse City, and lobbying hard in Lansing for better roads. His monument stands sixteen feet high, a pyramid composed of boulders upon which the names of all 83 Michigan counties are inscribed. Each boulder was carefully chosen to represent the character of its county—an iron-rich stone from Gogebic County in Michigan's Upper Peninsula and a rock with a chrome

Crowd watching early Cherry Festival parade on Union Street

embellishment from Wayne County, home of the auto industry, for examples. The *Traverse City Record-Eagle* gave frequent accounts of the stones arriving at Traverse City's Pere Marquette railroad station and the dedication of the cairn—for that was what it was called—brought many visitors to town, a suitable response to a monument honoring tourism by automobile.

The resort trade quickly responded to the automobile. When summer visitors came by train and boat, they stayed at lodges and hotels for weeks or months. Sometimes whole families resided at one location for the whole summer. The Neahtawanta Inn on Old Mission Peninsula and the Pennington Hotel in Interlochen were such resorts, enjoying success at first, but losing out over time to motels, which consisted of cottages and rooms let out by the night. Located along major highways, they commonly possessed a kitchen and a bathroom, making it possible for motorists to fix their own meals inexpen-

sively. Furthermore, they were located in scenic places far from city hotels—and they had their own parking.

Cars changed Northern Michigan. First, a new kind of travel—tourism—achieved popularity. No longer staying for weeks at one place, visitors would stay no more than a night or two at a single location before driving off to see a new sight. Rest and relaxation were less important than new experiences, new things to see, new things to buy. Second, visitors could reach Northern Michigan not just in the summer, but all year around. There were the flowers of spring, the usual summer attractions, the colorful leaves in the fall, and skiing in the winter. The tourist trade was not a seasonal occupation like cherry farming; it offered income in every month.

Traverse City responded rapidly to the new technology of the automobile. It added a splendid Miniature City attraction to Clinch Park, showcasing models of important local buildings made out of wood. Already a small zoo and aquarium occupied a site near Cass Street and the river, modest attractions for summer crowds of visitors. With the new beach, a bathhouse, lawns, and tree plantings of the park, Traverse City displayed its heightened interest in catering to auto-tourists.

Its passion for tourism went farther than the building up the bay front. In 1928, playing up the local cherry industry, Traverse City inaugurated the first Cherry Festival, organizing a splendid parade, selecting a Cherry Queen to represent the industry, scheduling a regatta with outboard motor races, a band concert featuring the National High School Band, and a Mummers parade with participants in wild and crazy costumes. The *Traverse City Record-Eagle* reported that thirty thousand spectators lined the parade route cheering the floats and bands. Although rain ruined the Mummers parade in the evening, the festival was deemed a grand success by city leaders and visitors alike.

By 1930 its celebration was not aligned to the actual cherry harvest (that typically occurred two weeks afterwards) so that the festival was primarily designed to bring visitors to the city for summer fun. It marked the beginning of the summer season. In years to come it would expand to eight days of frenzied events, as many as three parades, and aerial displays by the Blue Angels, the Navy exhibition squadron of jet fighters, and local events such as frog jumping contests, races among boats improvised from empty milk containers, and rubber ducky flotillas. Crowds of more than a hundred thousand people would gather by the shores of West Bay to watch the spectacular fireworks at the close of the festival.

Not all stories told of the twenties and thirties reflected a secure, prosperous, and tolerant community. The economy, after all, was in shambles—even before the effects of the Great Depression spread to Northern Michigan. Unemployed men stayed at home, ashamed they could not provide for their families. Wages were still low—as compared to other cities in Michigan and elsewhere—and conditions at the Indian settlement at Peshabestown had not changed, with poverty and alcoholism taking their toll on a proud people. It wasn't just the economy that troubled the community, but something more insidious: racism.

August 9,1924, 8:00PM: three explosions were detonated, one after the other, behind the Lyric Theater downtown. Panicked theatergoers and store

Cottages available for rent, Indian Trails Motel

patrons streamed outside to the Front Street sidewalks, wondering the cause. Shortly before the blasts, a burning cross was noted on Cass Street near the northern bridge over the Boardman River. At the same time, as many as twenty-five smaller flaming crosses were erected at street intersections around town by unnamed individuals. Finally, a car with four robed and hooded figures drove through downtown displaying an illuminated sign that spelled K. K. K. The Klan had arrived in Traverse City.

The Ku Klux Klan reached the peak of its power and influence across the country in the mid-twenties. It was not just anti-black, but anti-immigrant, anti-Semitic, and anti-Catholic as well. Traverse City had few minorities at the time—a small Jewish community, the tribe of Indians centered at Peshabestown in Leelanau County, and a moderate population of Bohemians and Poles who worked in manufacturing plants and on farms in the area. However, it had a large number of Catholics and supported two Catholic schools: St. Francis and Immaculate Conception.

A rally opposing parochial schools was held at the City Opera House on the Monday after the bombing. Public schools were better, according to Klansmen, but only if they adopted the "Americanism" they approved. Behind Klan activity in Traverse City, the conflict between Protestants and Catholics, largely invisible to the public eye, must have played an important part.

A suspect, Basil B. Carleton, was arrested in connection with the bombings behind the Lyric Theater. A jury decided that, although he had purchased dynamite recently and was seen coming from the site of the explosions, there was not enough evidence to convict since he was not caught in the act of detonation. Determined to arrest him on a lesser charge, the city prosecutor charged him with unlawful detonation of explosives, but this effort failed to get a conviction, too. Carleton left town a free man.

Eventually the Ku Klux Klan became deeply unpopular both locally and nation-wide. Beatings, cross-burnings, and detonations of dynamite turned people against the movement even as it self-destructed through scandals in the highest levels of Klan leadership. At its peak the KKK had 70, 000 members within the State of Michigan with large numbers in Detroit and other large cities in the southern half of the Lower Peninsula. Traverse City was not alone in its flirtation with intolerance and prejudice at this time in its history.

Prejudice can be expressed in ways less dramatic than bombs. It can be expressed by restaurants not serving blacks, by hotels not offering them lodging, by tourism advertisements boasting a population that is 95% native-born, by refusing to allow Jews to occupy certain neighborhoods, and by posting a sign outside the local country club stating "Gentiles Only." All of these contemptible actions were carried on by residents of the Traverse City area: among minorities, the town was regarded as off limits, a place to be avoided. The few surviving abolitionists who had fought the in the Civil War must have been surprised at the rise of Jim Crow attitudes among their children and grandchildren.

Changes

During the period 1910 to 1940 Traverse City began to take on a look that is familiar to us at the outset of the twenty-first century. Roads were paved, sidewalks poured, and trees planted in residential neighborhoods. Weekly garbage pickups reduced unsightly trash, discouraging rats, gulls, and crows from city residence. The Boardman River came to be seen as an asset rather than a means to dispose of sewage and other waste. People wanted to feel good about how their city looked—not just to bring in more summer tourists but to provide a pleasant living environment for themselves and for their children.

Traverse City had dreams of its future. One of those dreams featured the new Park Place building, erected in 1929, a miniature skyscraper of ten stories with a revolving beacon at the top as well as a pencil beacon that pointed to the nearby airport on top of Boughey Hill. In the thirties people had a feeling that air travel would amount to something, though they were not sure how to encourage it: a finger of light pointing at the airport seemed like a possibility. The larger revolving beacon was designed to improve navigation on Grand Traverse Bay, though its real purpose was to proclaim the importance of the city to all visitors approaching by car or train. With 2.5 million candlepower, it outshone the beacon on the Palmolive Building in Chicago. (In recent years the Park Place beacon has been replaced by a modern light not especially known for its brightness.)

The city boasted its modernity. As early as 1926 traffic signals on Front Street were automatically activated, an advance few cities could boast. The waterfront was no longer an industrial wasteland, but a park visitors could enjoy free from smoke and odors that characterized it only a decade or two before. The river was clean enough to drink out of (or nearly so). Postcards of the Park Place insisted it was "European"—surely a reference to its sophistication and elegance.

In fact, the city had a long way to go before it would attain its goal of sophistication. It boldly advertised in magazines that its population was "95% native-born," a hint that blacks and other minorities did not live there. Indeed it was white with a small Native American population—and for that reason its culture lacked the diversity and vibrancy of Lansing or Kalamazoo. It had no college, so its youth left town for Ann Arbor, East Lansing, Mount Pleasant, or Kalamazoo to secure their educations, though the National Music Camp at Interlochen began to attract the interest of young musicians.

The business district on Front Street began to take on the appearance of business districts all over the country as large chain stores replaced local stores present for decades. The Hannah and Lay Department Store closed all departments except hardware in 1929; Steinberg's Department store had closed eight years earlier. Penney's and Montgomery Wards filled the void—along with Woolworth's and Kresge's. By 1940 a brand-new Kroger's supermarket (later A&P) opened along Front Street, enticing customers away from local mom-and-pop grocery stores. Out of loyalty, many customers stuck with their local grocer, but they frequently went to a chain store when prices were too good to pass up.

Automobiles expressed residents' desire to participate in the twentieth century. Beyond conveying people where they wished to go, cars implied a wholesale change in values: they were fast and sexy. Newly emancipated women drove them not just on errands but for fun: it was the modern thing to do. Dating changed with the automobile: Before, men were required to visit women friends at the woman's home under the circumspect eye of her parents, but with an auto, he could pick her up and they could go dancing—or even drinking (illegally during Prohibition!). Cars represented an assault on traditional morality.

Since the early days of settlement, residents of the Traverse area were strongly Republican, accepting that party's stand on morality and temperance while rejecting the Democrats appeal to Dixie racism and the urban clamor of labor, immigrants, and Catholics. But citizens could be pushed too far in support of Big Money: in 1912 Grand Traverse County—along with the State of Michigan as a whole—voted for the Progressive Theodore Roosevelt, rejecting Republican Robert Taft. Later, in the throes of the Great Depression, people voted for Franklin Delano Roosevelt for president in two successive elections (1932 and 1936), the only times before or since that the County had supported a Democrat.

Why did Grand Traverse County—and all of Northern Michigan—support the Republican Party? After the Civil War the Republican Party was dominant throughout the Northern States; Civil War veterans remembered Lincoln and cast their ballots for his party for the rest of their lives. Republicans were for the native-born, farmers, small businessmen, leaders of industry, and churchgoers. They took strong moral positions—on temperance, in particular—and were regarded as more patriotic than Democrats. Locally, Republicans had far better organization and could get out the vote when an election called for that effort. In later years of the twentieth century, the Traverse City area seemed attractive to those who were angry at racial conflict in Southern Michigan. Some moved north to escape race-based crime, riots, and what they saw as bias against whites. By and large, they were Republicans.

Some values remained unchanged from previous decades. Education was still valued and school enrollment continued to climb in Traverse City. As compared to earlier times, schools were changing both in architecture and curriculum. In 1934 the oldest building at Central High school burned to the ground. With the help of stimulus money offered by the Federal government, a splendid new building was constructed for Junior High and elementary students. Its design reflected new attitudes towards education.

The new Junior High had a large study-library, a sound-proof band room, a well-equipped science room, a room for art and a sewing and fitting room, while the elementary school had a special room for special needs children, a room for deaf children, an elementary science and nature study room, and a physical education and recreation room. No longer was education solely aimed at students who enjoyed book learning: it was for all students, handicapped or not, college bound or not. The community was proud of its new school.

Between 1910 and 1940 Traverse City residents began to insist that the land and water should be restored, that officials should begin the arduous task of undoing the damage caused by logging and industry. Not only did they clean up the beach along West Bay and stop pouring raw sewage into the river, but they embarked on a tree planting program, both in town and on city-owned Brown Bridge property. At the latter location seventy-five men planted a forest of red and white pine, the "first municipal forest in the Middle West" according to the *Record-Eagle*. It was a belated atonement for the depredations of loggers in the nineteenth century.

The entire community embraced one unifying belief: the Traverse area had something special, that it stood apart from other communities in its natural beauty and in its people. No doubt many cities, towns, and villages feel the same way about their own communities—and with some justification since people everywhere work to make their neighborhoods attractive places to bring up children. But Traverse City, in its isolation from "downstate" (local usage of the term connoted wealth, power, and foreignness), was different and—dare anyone say it?—*better* than other places. Most families lived in Northwest Michigan at economic sacrifice. They could make more money elsewhere, yet they stayed in Traverse City. Was that the underlying reason for affirming the goodness of the community? That sacrifice implied something good enough to sacrifice for?

Entrance to Clinch Park at Cass Street about 1940

CHAPTER FOUR

The Making of a Modern City
1940-1970

Clinch Park: August, 1953

The freighter was unloading coal at the dock closest to Traverse City Light and Power's power plant. The sight impressed a few visitors and residents because it was rare: a large boat venturing so far south into Grand Traverse Bay. Older residents remembered well the waterfront when it daily presented a scene of work and bustle with steamers carrying both freight and passengers frequenting the old dock, now gone. In 1953 the Bay represented something very different from the world of work: it was about play.

With its expansive lawns and planted trees, Clinch Park had been cleaned up years before, but new things had been added since that early effort. Two great wheels joined together with a sturdy axle beckoned the curious—who were surprised to learn they were designed to drag heavy logs out of the woods. A bathhouse stood near the water inviting the young and brave to swim in water too cold for sensible people to enter. Nearby, a scale model of Traverse City made of wood attracted a score of visitors as they made out familiar buildings of the town: the Hannah and Lay building only two blocks away, the City Opera House across from it, and the Traverse City State Bank whose dome still shone at Union and Front Street.

A small building, the Con Foster museum, laid out antiques, relics and artifacts for all to see with stuffed owls sharing space with Indian wigwams, old muskets with crosscut saws, geodes with oxen yokes, Victorian costumes with fish nets. From the outside the building reflected a late interest in Art Deco, while on the inside it resembled Grandma's attic. The very young especially enjoyed the atmosphere since the unpredictable juxtapositions delighted and surprised them the most.

Near the museum was an aquarium and zoo built years before. Leaving exotic fishes for the magnificent Shedd Aquarium of Chicago, Traverse City's aquarium displayed local fish: walleye, perch, brown and brook trout, steelhead, large and small-mouth bass, and magnificent—and frightening—northern pike with their jaws full of sharp teeth. The cold glass walls of the fish tanks glistened with condensation in the summer and people lingered inside to escape the summer's heat. Nearby, the zoo emphasized the same theme: local animals as opposed to exotics (though peacocks strutted up and down uttering ear-shattering calls heard all over town). For the enlightenment of visitors, animal names were given in English and Odawa, a reminder of the people who lived with them first in this place.

In summer the most interesting exhibits were the visitors, themselves. Most of them came from "downstate," the term locals used for the prosperous southern-most four rows of counties. With the building of good roads and reliable automobiles, they flocked north in the summer, sometimes coming only for a weekend, arriving late Friday and heading home Sunday afternoon. As a consequence of this weekly migration, northbound lanes were jammed on Fridays and the southbound jammed on Sundays. Apparently, though, the traffic did not seem to bother people enough to keep them to home. The clean air, clean water, pleasant sunsets, moderate temperatures of summer overwhelmed their instincts to stay in Detroit, Lansing, Grand Rapids, or Kalamazoo—and, besides, they had money to spend.

Michigan was growing in population and wealth. Even auto plant workers could afford summer vacations for the family, hunting and fishing trips, and excursions to see autumn leaves. Some could even afford ownership of a cabin on a lake. Northern Michigan, though it was isolated from manufacturing downstate, could share in the wealth generated there. Indeed, on every weekend, it did.

The beacon atop the Park Place could be seen for miles as drivers approached the city late Friday night. For many, it signaled rest and peace, a life free of traffic, work deadlines, and the dirty air they were compelled to endure over the work week. They imagined retiring in the north, fishing and hunting, enjoying bright days and crisp nights without the pressures of earning a living weighing them down. In years to come many would pursue their dream and settle in the area.

Challenges

In 1940 change was in the air. Registration for the draft was inaugurated that year as events in Europe predicted possible United States intervention. The nation was still immersed in the Great Depression, but new ideas such as Social Security, the Work Progress Administration, and banking reform

"Miniature City" at Clinch Park

had been implemented years before. In Traverse City one note of progressive change was struck in the city's adoption of a city manager form of government. Amid accusations of mismanagement of city funds, residents narrowly approved the new system in a close election. City managers are hired by the city commission to run the city on a practical basis, devoting special attention to the city budget. By rejecting the older mayoral system residents decided in favor of clean, transparent financial conduct. The system remains with us to this day.

The Second World War brought immediate challenges to the Traverse area. For one thing, with local men serving in uniform, there were not enough workers to bring in the cherry crop. Growers got help however they could: they had buses bring townspeople to the orchards to earn a few dollars for a day's labor; they enlisted the help of the Women's Land Army, a Workers

Progress Administration program, to pick the cherries; they had a contingent of interned Japanese-Americans join the harvest; they even invited boys from the Lansing reformatory to come. It was not enough.

In 1943, 1600 Jamaicans joined work crews, soon joined by an army of Mexican migrant pickers. This diverse body of workers got the job done that year—as it would for next two war years. After the war migrants played an important role in harvesting fruit, though, with the advent of mechanical cherry harvesters (shakers), the number of workers declined drastically by the late sixties and early seventies. Still, at the outset of the 21st century, migrants do much farm labor locally, cutting asparagus early, then picking strawberries, sweet cherries, apples, and plums until mid-fall. Some of them settled here, providing a small measure of racial and ethnic diversity to the native (mostly white) population.

A challenge extending beyond the war years was the widely-held image of Northern Michigan as a region lacking in cultural amenities such as a symphony, a theater, a first-rate museum, as well as venues for good movies, concerts, ballet, and opera. Students left the area to attend college and—if they returned at all—went back to a community without the cultural assets of the college town they left. Hunting and fishing were not sufficient pastimes to earn their allegiance: they wanted educational advantages, concerts, good movies, and ethnic food. The city had to remake its image from a culturally barren town of the Northern Lower Peninsula to a vibrant place with an exciting variety of things to do.

If the young wanted diversity and excitement, many retirees coming to the area wanted a good hospital. Munson Hospital, first conceived by James Decker Munson as a satellite of Traverse City State Hospital, began in a small frame building still standing (at this date) at the corner of Eleventh and Elmwood Streets. In 1925 a modern brick facility was completed which served the needs of 55 patients, but by the end of the Second World War, Munson became severely overcrowded as new medical specialties and a burgeoning population placed stress upon the old building. Compared to new facilities downstate, the local hospital lagged in up-to-date laboratories, surgeries, and the latest medical technology. If Traverse City was to attract retirees—many with medical problems—it would have to modernize the way it delivered medical services to the elderly and to the resident population.

The economy, of course, was always a challenge. Workers still lamented, "A view of the Bay is worth half the pay," a refrain that carried over from earlier periods of history. Realizing large industry would not invest in the area, the local Chamber of Commerce pushed for small companies to move here, touting the region's lower labor costs and relatively less expensive land suitable for industrial development. At the same time, the Chamber continued to nurture the tourist trade, now dependent upon the automobile. In good times or bad, tourists kept the economy afloat.

The Traverse area had survived the "bad years" of the twenties and thirties, but it still had to work at overcoming the inherent disadvantage of its isolated location at the end of a long peninsula. It had made peace with that reality and played its assets for all to see: a clean, natural environment, a tranquil small town atmosphere, freedom from the hubbub of traffic and noise characterizing "downstate,"—and, though at this time it was seldom spoken aloud—the absence of conflict in a racially homogeneous society. The absence

Munson Hospital, 1955

of cultural and racial diversity was hardly seen as a problem at this time, but, in fact, it would become one. As barriers preventing mixing of people fell, the white, blue-collar culture of Traverse City would have to become more accepting of different colors, different ethnicities, and different religions. In future years it would achieve this unexpressed goal—even if it boasted about its ethnic purity as late as the thirties and forties.

Responses

For many years city leaders had wished to make Traverse City an educational center of the region. In the Lower Peninsula there were no four-year colleges north of Big Rapids and Mount Pleasant, a situation that drove many young people away from the area after graduation from high school. In fact, after World War I the state legislature had authorized the establishment of a Normal School in the city, but had neglected to appropriate funds. At the end of WWII, business and school leaders thought it was time to build a new community college even if they would build it themselves, without state aid.

After all, previously the energy of the city had been mobilized in the cleanup of Clinch Park in the thirties with citizens, rich and poor, gathering with hoes and pickups, to move stones, remove debris, and create a pleasant landscape. Upon the failure of a bond proposal aimed at creating a new park, they acted to make something happen through their own efforts. With the new college, they would do the same thing.

Such a venture requires leaders to organize fund-raising campaigns, convince the community of the worthiness of the project, and identify other dynamic figures willing to do the actual work. One such leader was Les Biederman, the owner and manager of Traverse City's first radio station, WTCM. Biederman, a brash young man eager to make changes in his adopted city of Traverse City, first encouraged Con Foster to construct a fine museum at Clinch Park. Following that, he devoted himself to the expansion and renovation of Munson Hospital, using his position in the local Chamber of Commerce and in the bully pulpit of his radio station to solicit funds from citizens and businesses. Upon completion of that goal, he was ready to tackle the community college problem.

The first roadblock was a state law that prohibited communities smaller than 25,000 people to build and operate such a college. In response to that challenge Arnell Engstrom, local representative to the Michigan legislature, had that restriction removed by authoring Bill 380 and moving it through the legislative process. After it was passed, all that remained was—to build the college.

That was a problem not easily solved. Biederman believed that a bond issue that fell on local taxpayers might fail and sought to gather funds the way he did with the hospital—through a vigorous fund-raising campaign. In short order his Founders Club enlisted businesses eager to support the college. Grocer Gerald Oleson sponsored a "Fisharee," an event that had fishermen donate ten cents an inch for every trout caught in his fish ponds south of town. And the Independent Grocers Alliance donated a penny for every loaf of bread bought.

Contributions were not limited to businesses: citizens groups helped, too. One of them held a dance at the Park Place and gave the proceeds to the cause and another gave the house receipts to a performance of *Peter Pan* to the college fund. Townspeople wanted their college.

One common practice of successful entrepreneurs is to start before you are ready. In accordance with that principle the college sprang up in the same year it was authorized. One day Les Biederman noticed unoccupied rooms in the city-owned airport terminal building. It occurred to him that those spaces could provide classroom space for the new college. After frantic preparations, on September 17, 1951, students assembled there to hear school superintendent Glenn Loomis welcome them to the new school. Without a decent library, without teaching materials, without a set curriculum, without a support staff of administrators, without all of the seemingly necessary accoutrements of post-high school education, the school opened for sixty-five newly enrolled students. Surely they must have harbored doubt as well as hope as their school year began.

In the beginning Northwestern Michigan College—the name selected for the new school—was opened under the authority of the Traverse City Public Schools. A problem presented itself with this arrangement: Northwestern Michigan College attracted students from a five-county area while the Traverse City Public Schools collected property tax for its support within its own district. As a result, over the first several years of its operation, the college became a financial burden to the public schools. The solution lay in new legislation from Lansing that provided for a Board of Directors to administer the school and a means of funding the school through a district-wide millage.

A college cannot exist in a few rooms at the city airport. From the start, Les Biederman and other forward-thinking leaders realized that the community college would need a campus of its own. Consequently, the funding arm of the college, Educational Fund, Inc., purchased land at the present campus location north of Front Street and east of Milliken Drive. With other lands acquired since that purchase date of 1951, the college had plenty of room for expansion. In addition, the aged white and red pines provided an appropriate background for a college founded in the north woods.

In the spirit of make-do, the college moved abandoned Coast Guard dormitories to the new campus in 1953. The frame buildings were disassembled at the airport and reassembled on site with local businesses and individuals helping with donation of materials, construction and painting. With the buildings completed after nearly two years of struggle, the college packed up its equipment and supplies and left the airport in March of 1955. Students and instructors—not professional movers—loaded twelve trucks and drove them to the new campus. It was how things got done at that time.

The first mission statement of the college speaks to the idealism of the school's founders:

> We, the people of northwestern Michigan with faith in each other, in our children, their future, and that of this beautiful country; knowing that knowledge and education is necessary to the progress and happiness of mankind do hereby unite in

Moving sign to new campus: 1955 photo showing students moving sign to new Northwestern Michigan College campus

joint effort in the formation of Northwestern Michigan College to serve the educational need of all our people regardless of age, race, creed and economic status; a college giving guidance and counseling for youth and adults, at the college or in their own homes and communities, creating a personal interest to improve themselves through their own efforts.

Here the pride of the community shines for all to see: We are creating this thing and it is good. In coming decades, from this small beginning, the college campus would grow to fill the wooded area it began to occupy in 1955. It would later develop two separate campuses in the Traverse area, the Boardman campus on Boardman Lake and the Maritime campus on West Bay. Enrollment would climb to more than 5000 students, not including the hundreds of citizens who took courses in extended education for no credit. The vision of Les Biederman achieved a reality even he would have marveled at.

Joe Maddy had a vision, too. A musician and music educator, he imagined a national orchestra made up of the best high school musicians. They would meet at a summer camp, practice together, and play before the world in live performances and radio broadcasts. The National High School Orchestra he organized and conducted was exactly what he envisioned: now he had to find it a home. To realize his dream he was not a person to wait for help from anyone: he simply made it happen—and practically overnight.

Rejecting a site in Maine, he discovered a failing resort in Northern Michigan near the village of Interlochen. It had frontage on two lakes and was surrounded by a gorgeous forest of pines and hardwoods: in its isolation from the currents of civilization it was a perfect place for a music camp. With a wizard in business named Charles Tremaine, he finagled a contract from resort owner Willis Pennington giving Pennington the exclusive contract to supply meals to campers. In the end, the campers would pay for the camp! Later, the same principle operated when Maddy had "scholarship" cabins constructed and rented out. Creating the means by which loans would pay themselves off, he could direct rental proceeds to scholarships for deserving musicians.

Scarcely a year elapsed from the time Maddy's vision was first sketched out to when the first camp opened in 1928. With his connections to music educators, instrument makers, and businessmen, he was able to supply the needs of 22 faculty members and 115 campers that first year. As with Northwestern Michigan College, the principle "Start before you are ready" operated to create an infant enterprise which would later grow into something magnificent.

Without promotion, the experiment might have died still-born, but Maddy knew better. He made connections with colleges, especially with the University of Michigan, to establish a college-level camp unit, arranged for broadcasts on national radio networks NBC and CBS, and even saw to it a movie featuring the Music Camp was made: *There is Magic in Music* (1941). The camp survived the Great Depression (unlike other such camps) and was poised to expand in the 1940's.

Then the hammer fell. First, the War drained the body of potential students. Added to that, Joe Maddy ran afoul of the American Federation of Musicians for his airing broadcasts with young, non-union affiliated musicians. The National Music Camp was blacklisted by the union—union members could not teach at the facility. Though not anti-union, Maddy protested the blacklisting by enlisting non-union faculty at colleges and universities to teach the campers. For fifteen years union musicians avoided teaching at Interlochen, a terrible blow to the prestige of the camp. Finally, after discussion with the musicians union, the ban was lifted in 1958.

The 1950's saw prosperity return to the National Music Camp. New buildings were constructed and old buildings remodeled, debts were paid off, and school enrollment reached new highs. Instead of resting on his laurels, Joe Maddy set about to realize one of his oldest dreams: the establishment of a year-around Arts Academy.

The road was tortuous leading to his goal. The National Music Camp board had to agree to construction—and the board was made up of many members opposed to incurring more debt. There was simply not enough money to begin a new expensive project like an Arts Academy. An immense fundraising effort would have to be made—and that, itself, would cost money.

Maddy's reply to these objections was to place plumbing underground and to construct two weatherized dormitories, Beethoven and Brahms. In 1960 board members were startled to find a deep hole dug in the ground, the basement for another winterized dormitory. It looked as if the Academy was coming whether the board approved it or not.

At this time several board members opposing Maddy's project retired or were eased out of their positions; they were replaced by persons supportive of the new school. The final objection to the Academy went down when Clement Stone, philanthropist from Chicago, donated 350 thousand dollars towards construction. In the end he—and his foundation—would back the Interlochen Arts Academy many decades to come.

Early photo of The Bowl, Interlochen

With Stone's support, the board could resist no longer. In 1961 they authorized the charter that brought the Academy to life. It was to emphasize both the arts—all of them, not just music—and academic study with strong departments in literature, science, and mathematics. In 1963 the school opened with 132 students; two years later there were 300. In future years its reputation would soar both from its commitment to arts education and to academic achievement.

The final addition to the Interlochen complex was the founding of radio station WIAA in 1963. Patterned upon WUOM of Ann Arbor, the station became a charter member of National Public Radio (NPR) in 1970. From small beginnings—it broadcast only eight hours a day at first—it has grown to become an important cultural asset of the Traverse area. WIAA was the final achievement of Joseph Maddy, who died in 1966. His memory is preserved in the institutions he built.

At a smaller scale the arts flourished in Traverse City. When Elnora Milliken, sister-in-law of Governor William Milliken, arrived in the city in the early 1950's, she could not find an outlet for her musical talent since the area did not have symphony orchestra. With the same energy of Les Biederman and Joe Maddy, she resolved to build one, identifying supporters and musicians and pushing them to participate in her vision. So it was that she organized the Northern Michigan Symphony Orchestra, which presented its first concert in December, 1952. At first composed of community musicians, it evolved to become the only professional orchestra in the Northern Lower Peninsula, the Traverse Symphony Orchestra. The excellence of that body has been recognized by performers and conductors who perform in both national and international venues.

Elnora Milliken was responsible for another cultural asset of the Traverse community: the Old Town Playhouse. Displaying her customary enthusiasm, she joined with other interested citizens to create a community theater. In 1960 the Traverse City Civic Players presented their first drama, *You Can't Take It With You*, at the High School auditorium. After a time spent at the Park Place dome during the sixties, the Players purchased the Christian Church at the corner of Cass and Eighth Streets in 1975. It became known as the Old Town Playhouse and continues to offer a full schedule of plays for adults and children to this day.

Even before the Traverse City Civic Players Traverse City residents could enjoy good theater—at least in the summer. Ruth Bailey, a star of radio drama, started the Cherry County Playhouse in 1955, staging performances in a brightly striped tent across from the Park Place Hotel. One of the first professional theater companies in Michigan, it brought Hollywood stars to the city: Zasu Pitts, Joe E. Brown, Buddy Ebsen, Pat O'Brien, and Pat Paulsen. The Cherry County Playhouse moved across the street to the Park Place dome in the 1960's, continuing to bring plays to the town through 1990 at which time it moved to Muskegon, finally closing its doors at that location in 2003.

Munson Hospital began a period of phenomenal growth beginning in the 1950's. As the community grew, so did the hospital. At this time, the medical lab and maternity ward needed room to expand, even as new medical specialties (such as radiology) required space within the building. Expansions were added in 1952, 1958, 1960, and 1969—and still the hospital was too small.

From the beginning, James Decker Munson envisioned a hospital that would reach beyond the boundaries of Traverse City and its immediate environs. At the ground-breaking ceremony for the 1925 building, the *Traverse City Record-Eagle* expressed the hope that the new hospital will have "the capacity and facilities for handling medical cases from an entire region." That vision would be realized under the administration of John C. Bay, president of the Munson system from 1970 to 1993, who shepherded the transition of Munson from a community hospital to a regional healthcare provider.

Munson Healthcare, founded in 1985 under Bay's leadership, expanded medical services both inside and outside Traverse City: first, at the former

Osteopathic Hospital on Munson Avenue and, in later years, in Charlevoix, Kalkaska, Cadillac, Grayling, Gaylord, Frankfort, and Manistee. Munson Medical Center, the nucleus of James Decker Munson's 1925 General Hospital, is the largest component of Munson Healthcare with 391 beds, 3700 employees, 420 associated physicians, and 50 specialty services at the time of this book's publication (2013). Interestingly, the hospital has grown outward from the original building, forming a complex made up of numerous wings added throughout the years. From one walkway, it is still possible to read "Hannah-Lay Morgan" Pavilion upon an interior wall, a token of the time when Perry Hannah and A. Tracy Lay's influence on the town was widely remembered.

Changes

A demographic study of Traverse City conducted in 1974 sheds light on the citizens of Traverse City. The sample of one hundred households showed a median income of 10,500 dollars, a figure much in line with national figures at the time. The median education level was high school graduate, 12 years of schooling, pointing to a work force that was primarily blue-collar. Median household size was two persons, greatly differing from the national median of four persons. In the study, fully one person out of three was a newcomer to the Traverse City area.

This last figure is of particular interest. It underlines the fact that the population of Traverse City is not made up of descendants of early settlers, but is constantly changing as people arrive from other places. This observation explains much: the modern city of Traverse City cannot attribute its successes to strong pioneer stock, but neither can it lay its racism and provincialism to an unbroken line of narrow-minded families. The mix of citizens is constantly changing, for better or for worse.

The population of the Traverse City area grew considerably between 1940 and 1970 as it did throughout Michigan and the nation. Jobs grew, too, though the economic disparity between Southern Michigan and Northern Michigan continued. Low-paying jobs in tourism, fruit processing, and small business still reinforced the refrain, "A view of the Bay is worth half the pay," but at least the area was insulated from the ups and downs of the auto industry. In the late 1950's the state suffered a severe economic depression brought about by the auto industry's expansion of manufacturing into other states, reduction in employment by automation, and the shift of the federal government's defense expenditures from conventional armaments to missiles. With no auto plants, Traverse City was less affected than large manufacturing centers in Southern Michigan.

Newcomers to the city did not choose to reside within the city limits. In 1940 Grand Traverse County had 23,390 residents, 14,455 of whom lived in the city. By contrast, in 1990 the County had 64,273 residents, while the city had 15,155. Higher taxes for city residents, homes too small for growing families, a desire for country living, and cheap automobile transportation were factors that drove new arrivals to townships neighboring the city. At this time people throughout the United States were fleeing cities for the suburbs. New residents arriving in Traverse City were not exceptions.

Population growth outside the city implies an increase in auto traffic and urban sprawl. Grandview Parkway opened in 1953 to great fanfare as it allowed suburban residents to round West Bay at 35 miles per hour while affording them a "grand view" of the water. The thoroughfare was not welcomed by all since it cut off ready access to the Bay by city residents. The change of southern access to the city from Rennie Road (now Veterans Drive) to four-lane forty-mile-per hour Division Street had its critics, too. They pointed out that a busy highway through a residential neighborhood was more like "downstate" than peaceful Northern Michigan. The city was being hemmed in by rivers of cars carrying tourists, commuters, and shoppers to local businesses, schools, and the centers of government. The problem would only get worse in years to come. (At the time of this writing, voters approved a measure designed to reconfigure Division Street to make it more friendly to pedestrians and property owners.)

Schools had changed, too, over this period. Passed in 1964, a state law requiring school districts to offer a kindergarten-through-high school program set the stage for widespread consolidation of school districts. In 1970 the Traverse City Area Public Schools opened its new Junior High on West Silver Lake Road. Its enrollment of approximately 1800 students made it one of the largest in the state, a fact that troubled many in the community who remembered the smaller schools of their youth. Graduating classes became larger, too, growing from 294 in 1960 to 618 in 1974.

Traverse City Central High School offered a "comprehensive" academic program designed to serve all students, not just those thinking of a four-year college degree. In place of a college diploma, students could earn a general diploma emphasizing courses in industrial arts and business. Furthermore, those most at risk for dropping out before graduation could elect the Al Lock-man Outdoor Laboratory, a program conducted off-campus which taught such down-to-earth skills as practical carpentry, metal working, agriculture, and sawmill operations. A school-within-a-school, the Outdoor Lab was especially helpful to those students in danger of getting lost within an impersonal school environment serving more than 1800 students.

Local schools did not receive the support larger cities in Southern Michigan could provide. Compared to cities with large manufacturing plants nearby, Traverse City Area Public Schools received less money for every mil of property tax levied. As a result, schools were consistently underfunded, leaving little room for small class sizes, superior facilities, special programs, and adequate teacher salaries. At a time when local teachers were underpaid in comparison to other school districts, Traverse City teachers went out on strike in 1967 and 1979, with a day-long "sick-out" in 1977, but the militancy of teachers did little to bring local salaries in line with other districts better able to secure education funding. The state's adoption of Proposal A in 1994 did not improve the situation since higher funded school districts were "grandfathered in" at a higher level of state support than Traverse City. The disparity between rich downstate districts and Traverse City continues to this day (2013).

It is important to remember that much stayed the same in the Traverse City area over the period from 1940 to 1970. Native Americans lived this period as they did previously: in poverty and depression. From the outside, Pesha-bestown, located along scenic M22 in Leelanau County, presented little more than a church and a collection of run-down homes—an embarrassment to both Indians and whites alike, but from the inside, tribal members preserved native traditions through maintaining close ties to the land and waters—hunting, fishing, and practicing traditional arts and crafts. Ensuing decades would mark great changes in their lives.

Farmers had good crops and bad, Cherry Festivals came and went, tourists flooded in during the warm weather months and left for jobs and school after Labor Day. Downtown shopping on Front Street changed but little, though the banging of a distant drum—the spread of commerce outside the city's hub—could be heard in the distance. Traverse City State Hospital functioned as it had for eighty-five years, but something new was in the works. New drugs had helped schizophrenics live nearly normal lives and a movement was afoot to close large mental hospitals, replacing them with community mental health programs. That change would play itself out all over the United States in the next twenty years.

One thing would not change: the deeply felt feeling that Traverse City was an extraordinary place to live. The 1974 survey of people's attitudes towards life in Traverse City was unequivocal: 86 percent of respondents said they were "very satisfied" about living in the area. Nation-wide that figure stood at 74 percent. There was something special about living in this area, so far separated from others.

View of West Bay, 2012

Chapter Five

When History Touches the Present
1970-2013

Clinch Park: August, 2010

The sound of Grandview Parkway traffic overwhelms the softer sound of the waves against the steel sheet pilings defending the Open Space from the Bay. A concrete walkway overlooks the water with benches offered to those wishing to view the sail and motor boat traffic on the Bay. Nearby lawns and trees are attempting to recover from the impact of thousands of human feet impressed less than a month ago by Cherry Festival visitors. Alongside the walkway a few splendid yachts are moored, their owners onboard or absent—some of them attending a film shown at a venue of the Traverse City Film Festival. East of the Open Space, a giant inflatable movie screen stands upright, a few plastic chairs gathered in front awaiting occupants for the showing of the feature after dark.

Loungers and strollers hear the sounds of the beachfront in summer: a volleyball game in progress, the buzzing of one-manned watercraft on the Bay, children in distress and joy, and gulls crying in cacophony as they wheel above crowds of vacationers. The sights signify the season as well: drying swimmers, boaters in flip-flops and bright summerwear, iPhone manipulators, caregivers to children, readers, bikers, and sleepers. People celebrate the summer in diverse ways—as they always have.

The city bustles. A colorful hot-air balloon glides across the sky, its riders enjoying the panorama spread out below: the boats crowding the bayshore, the cityscape of the town with the Maritime Academy, the new parking deck on Front Street, the copper dome of Fifth Third Bank, and the lighthouse tower of the Park Place Hotel. Two schooners crisscross the Bay, the *Madeline* and the *Malabar*, taking summer visitors for afternoon sails. Closer to shore, motor-driven craft cluster by the beaches as amphibious people traffic between boat and land. The scene pleases the eyes of balloon riders: the world is represented in miniature below like the birds' eye view maps of the past, the traffic of boats and cars resembling toys in a museum diorama. From a distance, it appears that all is well.

Still, up close, there are things that bother: a brown slime covers rocks: algae that grows as an indirect consequence of Quagga and Zebra mussel invasion. The water level is low, nearly the lowest on record, and large boats with deep draft have trouble entering the marina. The Con Foster Museum stands empty, its odd collection of artifacts, having been moved to the old Sixth Street library. And the tracks of the miniature train, *The Spirit of Traverse City*, no longer circle Clinch Park—a loss for young children that enjoyed its clicking progress and shrieking whistle. Finally, the smell of auto and boat exhaust provides olfactory background much as the noise of traffic on Grandview Parkway interferes with the sounds of waves. There is a price for the success of Traverse City in the summer.

Whatever its shortcomings, the assets of the beachfront overwhelm people's sensibilities. This is a pleasant place to be—as it has been for many summers. People come to see the water, see each other, go swimming, play Frisbee, watch movies, and consume ice cream. They come to play in the warmth and beauty of the place.

Challenges

The growth of population and wealth in the Grand Traverse region presented a contradiction to its residents: they welcomed increased commerce, but resented the intrusions of visitors and newcomers upon their way of life. A simple trip across town required minutes of waiting at stoplights, even triggering occasional "gridlock" if undertaken during rush hour. In spring, favorite woodlands now sprouted new homes instead of mushrooms. Compared to former times, beaches were crowded with tourists during summer months. And such typically "downstate" crimes of burglary and violence seemed more common up north than before—at least in the minds of local residents.

Traffic, noise, air, and water pollution are associated with locally disparaged big cities of Southern Michigan, not Traverse City. How did the region address such problems as they made their appearance in this place so isolated from the currents of modernism? How did county and city officials regulate commercial and residential zoning, control urban sprawl, and provide transportation for those without automobiles? How effective was that response in addressing those problems? The answers to these questions do not receive final answers, only continued progress reports as the community enters the twenty-first century.

The conflict between economic development and environmental preservation played itself out in the creation of the Sleeping Bear Dunes National Lakeshore, a dramatic story that ended in 1970 with the establishment of the national park. That battle was not restricted to the dunes and their environs, however: it was carried on before zoning boards throughout the area—whenever the sacrifice of a natural area had to be weighed against commercial and residential development. City, township, and county officials were asked again and again: How can the economic benefits of development be balanced against environmental degradation and the loss of small-town atmosphere?

Population growth occurred primarily on the outskirts of Traverse City. Neighboring townships now held populations far greater than the city, itself. Commercial development ringed the city with the construction of malls and "Big Box" stores such as Meijers. How could downtown Traverse City compete with such powerful economic forces—especially when the city enjoyed no population growth at all?

A city without growth cannot collect tax revenues sufficient to support public assets such as a library, a zoo, a museum, or a waterfront park. Increasing taxes places too great a burden on city residents and cutting services diminishes the quality of life. How can Traverse City provide the advantages of cultural and recreational amenities while preventing an exodus of residents bound for surrounding townships where living costs are lower? That question, it turns out, was answered very differently for the public library and the Clinch Park zoo. Entering the twenty-first century, area residents still are grappling with this important issue.

For too long Indians of the area lived in poverty and misery in Peshabestown and other small towns of Northwest Lower Michigan. Only federal recognition of the tribe could provide tribal members with the legal standing to challenge state laws restricting hunting and fishing rights. How did the Grand Traverse Band of Ottawa and Chippewa Indians achieve tribal recognition? How did that recognition improve the lives of local Indians? In the decades between 1980 and 2000 a court decision—together with a bold program of development —would transform the lives of local tribal members.

Responses

The conflict between commercial and residential development and land preservation played out with special drama in the creation of the Sleeping Bear Dunes National Lakeshore. Beginning in 1959 and ending in 1970, Congress repeatedly introduced bills in the House of Representatives and the Senate to establish a new national park in Benzie and Leelanau Counties. Due to ineptitude in framing the bills and to poor communications with summer and year-around residents of the areas involved, ten years elapsed before the Lakeshore was finally approved. The story tells much about the people of Northern Michigan, their values and their deeply held convictions.

At first, inland lakes such as Glen Lake and Platte Lake were included within the proposed park boundaries. The perception of residents was that the federal government was initiating a "land grab," unfairly depriving home and summer cottage owners of their properties without consideration of the impact of a new National Park on local business, schools, roads, and governance. In short order a Citizens Council was formed to oppose the creation of the park under the leadership of Ove Johnson, a summer resident of Glen Lake. On August 31, 1961 the anger of citizens spilled out at a public meeting called to explain the proposal to local residents. As historian Theodore Karamanski stated, it was the day the Sleeping Bear National Lakeshore nearly died.

On that hot, humid evening between 1500 and 2000 year-around and summer residents gathered at the Glen Lake School gymnasium to hear Conrad Wirth, Director of the Park Service, outline plans for the park. Interrogated by Ove Johnson in hostile fashion, he could not provide answers to questions about a legislative bill in its first stage of formulation. Catcalls, jeers, and scornful laughter filled the auditorium as the crowd sensed Wirth was out of his element. The next day, the *Traverse City Record-Eagle* published a scathing editorial about the meeting. It began: "An appalling and almost unbelievable demonstration of how far bureaucratic planners in Washington can go in disregarding the people's rights in the name of the public welfare was given by Conrad L. Wirth, director of the National Park Service, at a public meeting on the proposed Sleeping Bear Dunes national recreation area Wednesday night…"

Michigan Senator Philip A. Hart's bill to establish Sleeping Bear died in the face of public opposition. However, the Senator did not give up. Three more bills authorizing the park would be offered before Congress finally passed HR18776, which was signed by President Richard M. Nixon to become law. With each successive failure, the legislation was improved, changing the name from "Recreation Area" to "National Lakeshore," eventually stripping out the inland lakes from park boundaries, assuring that property rights of landowners within the park will be respected, and offering quick and reasonable settlement of property sales.

Political opposition to Sleeping Bear evaporated because of changes involving two Republican lawmakers. When Congressman Robert Griffin, representative of Northern Michigan was appointed senator by Governor

George Romney in 1966, he no longer presented a barrier to the passage of Hart's legislation since he resigned his position as local representative to become senator. With Griffin gone, another Republican would need convincing: Guy R. Vander Jagt, the new representative.

Vander Jagt startled opponents of the park with his conversion to the cause. He indicated he would support the bill in exchange for assurances that Sleeping Bear property owners' rights would be respected and that a new four-lane highway would be built through his district. Upon hearing Vander Jagt's change of heart, the members of the Citizens Council of Leelanau and Benzie counties were outraged, but their protests fell upon deaf ears: VanderJagt would not change his mind. After the fuss had died down, Vander Jagt was able to say with pride, "Phil Hart is the father of the park; I might be the uncle or something like that."

What does the Sleeping Bear controversy tell us about the values of Northern Michigan residents? First, it shows an active antipathy for solutions imposed from the outside upon local people. Federal bureaucrats were despised for their disregard of locals, their arrogance, and their politics—since most were Democrats in a strongly Republican district. Second, residents expressed their concerns about commercial and residential development in a relatively pristine natural area. Neither full time residents nor summer visitors wanted housing developments obscuring pleasant vistas, ugly strip commercial developments, or honky tonk recreation facilities near Sleeping Bear. In the end, the best way to prevent ugly commercialism was to create a new federal park. In 1970 not all people agreed with that conclusion, but certainly a majority did—and now, after more than forty years, an overwhelming majority is grateful for the Sleeping Bear National Lakeshore.

The response of Traverse City to increased growth is laid out in city plans drawn up in 1942, 1962, 1977, 1994, and 2006. While the two earliest plans were mostly concerned with encouraging appropriate physical development of city land, later plans recognized the importance of environmental protection and maintaining a small-town atmosphere. In consonance with the Zeitgeist of the time, 1962 and 1977 plans advocated building downtown malls to compete with those certain to be built at the city's periphery. Later plans abandoned these proposals, concentrating on historic preservation, enhancing the riverfront and access to the Bay, and controlling growth.

Unlike earlier efforts, beginning in 1977, residents were asked to participate in writing planning goals.

The opposite of planned growth is urban sprawl. Traverse City, like most cities across the United States, was deeply afflicted with that problem, the center of commerce moving from downtown to Garfield Township in malls and strip developments during the 1970s. Traffic artery U.S. 31 and South Airport Road sprouted businesses like mushrooms in a wasteland unfriendly to pedestrians and bicyclists. The Traverse City Area Public Schools built new elementary schools in far-flung places, eventually constructing West Senior High School more than five miles from the city limits. Lots and houses were small inside the city limits, making the city less attractive to those with large families. According to the 2000 census, the average household size for owner-occupied units in the city was 2.31 as compared to 2.6 for Grand Traverse County. Children lived outside the city, primarily.

Traverse City and the surrounding region did not deal effectively with urban sprawl. Neighboring townships of Garfield and East Bay saw no reason to limit and control growth when increased valuations brought in more property tax. Gasoline was cheap—relative to other expenses at least into beginning of the twenty-first century—so newcomers flocked to the suburbs and beyond where housing and transportation expenses were low. The attractive dream home on five acres five miles from town beckoned newcomers to settle on former pastures and woodlots. That dream exerted a powerful influence on those escaping a crowded Southern Michigan with its attendant noise, dirt, and pollution.

Even if most newcomers desired suburban living and shopping, Traverse City downtown merchants were not going to sink into decline without a fight. In the sixties the Downtown Traverse City Association was formed to promote the interests of downtown stores by sponsoring events designed to bring shoppers downtown and by addressing problems shared by all merchants in the downtown area. In 1979 the city took advantage of a new state law authorizing the formation of a Downtown Development Authority (DDA), creating the first Tax Increment Financing (TIF) district located south of the Boardman River including much land formerly occupied by industry along Lake Street. A TIF district captures increased tax valuations as development proceeds in barren areas, enabling the DDA to proceed with more projects to bring more people downtown. In short order, apartments and condos began to spring up on ground thought to be industrial wasteland. At the same time public improvements such as public walkways, tree plantings along Front Street, and enhanced cityscapes appeared downtown. Traverse City was not going the way other cities had gone: it would not fade into a sorry collection of empty storefronts and trash-filled parking lots.

In 1997 a new TIF district was created from the northern boundary of the first TIF district to the bay shore. With this expanded power the DDA continued to combat urban decay. Notably, it addressed the downtown parking problem with the building of the Larry C. Hardy parking deck between Front and State Streets. That structure, together with the Old Town parking deck, enabled Hagerty Insurance to invest heavily in downtown, making the city its corporate headquarters. With good jobs arriving to the downtown area, a lively streetscape of fine restaurants, theaters, and concert venues blossomed along Front Street.

One source of downtown prosperity is the revived State Theater on the 200 block of Front Street. Long a film house—its predecessor, the Lyric opened its doors in the twenties—the State became a community art theater. Filmmaker Michael Moore sparked its rebirth, offering his organizational skills, contacts with filmmakers, and personal funds to restore the physical presence of the theater and to create the Traverse City Film Festival (TCFF).

Depending upon an enormous staff of volunteers, the first festival in 2005 showed 31 films in 52 screenings, selling 50 thousand tickets. Six years later the TCFF offered 156 screenings with 128 thousand admissions. Drawing visitors from all over the world, it provided a boost to the downtown business at the end of July and beginning of August. The crowd the TCFF attracted was different from that of the Cherry Festival. Appealing to a mix of ages, it drew filmgoers who cared about foreign films, independent films, documentaries, and little heralded "sleepers." Panel discussions with stars, directors, and writers brought thousands of people to the City Opera House, the State Theater, and to other theater venues throughout the city. Traverse City, for at least a week, became cosmopolitan.

From the beginning, the State Theatre has served local residents. It offers free admission for community events like high school state championship football games, political debates, the annual Michigan/Michigan State football game, and other events of state and national interest. Remembering the 25-cent ticket price of the early Lyric theater, it charges a quarter for Wednesday matinees. Besides its reasonable prices, the theater is stunningly beautiful

Residential development along the Boardman River

from its flashing bulbs in the marquis, its comfortable seats, richly appointed wall decorations, and the starry sky depicted on the ceiling. It has become one of the finest theaters in Michigan and in the nation.

The State Theater could not have happened through the efforts of Michael Moore alone. From the start it depended on the efforts of hundreds of volunteers, not just for the TCFF but for the daily operations of the theater.

State Theater at night, early 1950s

Overhead costs are kept low by offering individual memberships and business partnerships and by inviting citizens to donate labor—from selling tickets to making popcorn. The support of the community in maintaining the State should remind the reader of the building of Clinch Park in the thirties: then as now Traverse City functions as a community with shared interests and values.

The development of Traverse City's West Bay sheds light onto the nature of the forces that shape the city and the values that residents wish to proclaim in public spaces. In contrast to Traverse Citians of the 1930's who wished to attract tourists with a museum, a miniature city, a zoo, and an aquarium, modern residents wanted open space, an unobstructed view of West Bay. With four-lane Grandview Parkway opening in 1953, commuters enjoyed views of the Bay more than city residents did. By contrast, holding sun screen and ice chests, beach goers crossed the busy highway at risk to their lives. In future years planners would attempt to undo the harsh severing of the bay front from the lives of citizens, by suggesting tunnels for pedestrians, overpasses, and traffic-slowing techniques. So far, they have not been very successful in reconnecting the city with the Bay.

With tax revenues scarcely increasing as growth occurred outside the city, Traverse City had to make hard choices with regard to maintaining cultural and recreational assets. Clinch Park became open space with mowed grass and trees dominating an area once filled with tourists. Its zoo was abandoned because of its expense and the opposition of residents to living conditions provided for the animals. At the same time, the Clinch Park Marina was expanded, providing more mooring places for visiting yachts. A recent effort to rethink the Bay plan resulted in the construction of a bathhouse, a splash pond for children, and a kayak and boat rental facility, but city residents expressed a strong preference for keeping the area free of development at forums designed to capture public input. The waters of the Bay were primarily seen first as a pleasant vista and second as an attraction for tourists and a recreational site for residents.

Unlike the city zoo, the Traverse City Public Library was able to cope with reduced operating money. It sought regional funding, becoming the Traverse Area District Library in 1983. In September of that year the library attempted to pass a millage, but failed in that effort 2936 to 2694 with residents from outlying areas strongly opposing a tax that would not benefit them. Unfazed by that defeat, library supporters put a similar measure on the ballot scarcely two months later, and won this time, though outlying residents again expressed their opposition.

Faced with a tiny library building serving an expanding population, the Traverse Area District Library realized a new facility would have to be built. A twenty-year bond proposal to build a new library passed handily in 1996, providing resources for the construction of a new library off Woodmere Avenue. By the large margin of approval obtained for the bond, township residents showed they were not opposed to a library millage as long as their own satellite library received its fair share of resources. As with Northwestern Michigan College, regional support had enabled the institution to thrive in tight economic times as the city budget continued to fall short.

The construction of a new library left the old Carnegie building on Sixth Street empty. After a renovation campaign it was reborn as the Grand Traverse Heritage Center, the successor to the Con Foster Museum formerly located at Clinch Park. With the city in dire financial straits efforts were made to cut off city funding for the history museum. At the time of this writing the future of the Traverse City History Center (the name of the institution now comprised of the archives of the Historical Society and the Con Foster collection) is unclear.

Historic buildings in need of restoration abounded within the city. The population of the Traverse City State Hospital, after reaching a peak of 3600 patients in 1966, declined to 140 at its closing. Its campus was filled with decrepit buildings covered with lead-based paint, their roofs sagging and letting in snow and rain. Inevitably, the State of Michigan declared they should be demolished, sending a crew with demolition equipment to the site to accomplish the job. They were met by a party committed to keep the buildings standing, the Coalition for Logical Land Use. After discussion, the wrecking crew abandoned their plan, leaving the decaying buildings to the wind, snow, and rain. Something had to be done—and done fast—or else the weather would accomplish what humans had not been able to.

In 1990 the City of Traverse City and Garfield Township adopted an Adaptive Reuse Feasibility Plan for the State Hospital grounds, recommending preservation of most buildings. The Grand Traverse Redevelopment Corporation (GTRC) was established to oversee the preservation and redevelopment process and the state complied by transferring the land to the GTRC. The table was set for developers to submit their plans and save the buildings.

Only no one came to the table—at least until 2001 when the Minervini Group laid out a development plan that promised success. In good faith the Minervinis replaced the roof on Building 50, the oldest and largest building of all. Over the next decade the old hospital was transformed into a magnificent residential and commercial complex. As they did in 1885, the newly painted cupolas of the Italianate building still remind visitors of European elegance.

The GTRC disbanded in 2006, yielding to a new body, the Grand Traverse Joint Planning Commission, to carry out its mission of overseeing development on the Grand Traverse Commons grounds (the name referring to the large area including the historic barns, pastures, wetlands, and forests). At present the Botanical Gardens Society is planning to create a formal gardens, a learning center, and walking paths over the terrain Perry Hannah walked more than a hundred years before. At that time he was preparing to explain to Lansing lawmakers why Traverse City would be the most suitable location for a new mental hospital, emphasizing the restorative powers of nature for those troubled with mental illness. The hospital is gone, but even in the twenty-first century the land is still being used by citizens to find peace and tranquility in a noisy, busy, and sometimes trying world.

Indians living at Peshabestown had not enjoyed the relative prosperity of Traverse City during the 1960's and 1970's. Motorists driving through the settlement saw run-down homes—some with outdoor toilets—junked automobiles, litter, and other signs of rural poverty. High unemployment, crime and alcoholism afflicted the community as they had throughout the twentieth century. For years tribal leaders understood that the way out of poverty and despair lay in federal tribal recognition and the benefits that came with that status. Again and again the tribe sought recognition—in 1934, in 1943—failing both times for reasons that were not specified.

Finally, after federal policy changed to become more favorable towards tribal recognition, the tribe applied again in 1979. This time its petition was submitted under new federal guidelines and there was every expectation it would be approved. A year later, after submission of the formal request for recognition and a tribal constitution, the long sought-after goal was achieved: the Grand Traverse Band of Ottawa and Chippewa Indians was formally recognized by the United States Government as a tribal entity.

With recognition, the tribe could contest violations of hunting and fishing laws brought by the state of Michigan. Since 1974 Indian tribal member Art Duhamel had been cited five times for violating state fishing laws. In 1979 federal judge Noel Fox ruled that the Treaty of 1836, which granted Indian fishing and hunting rights, could not be ignored by modern officials. However, treaty rights only applied to federally recognized tribes: Judge Fox's ruling vindicated Art Duhamel after the federal government granted recognition.

Tribal recognition was important for another reason: it paved the way for casino gambling near Peshabestown and later in Acme township in Grand Traverse County. In 1984 the tribe opened the Super Bingo Palace and the Leelanau Sands Casino, the first high stakes bingo operation in Michigan. Moving to a better location in 1985, it began to attract hundreds of visitors drawn from the area as well as from places far away. Gaming operations increased eleven years later when the Grand Traverse Band built the Turtle Creek Casino near Acme, Michigan. In response to a challenge to the legality of that casino, Judge Douglas Hillman declared in support of the tribe's position:

In the fiscal year 2001 Turtle Creek provided approximately 89% of the Band's gaming revenue. The casino now employs approximately 500 persons, approximately half of whom are tribal members. Revenues from the Turtle Creek Casino also fund approximately 270 additional tribal government positions, which administer a variety of governmental programs, including health care, elder care, youth services, education, housing, economic development and law enforcement. The casino also provides some of the best employment opportunities in the region, and all of its employees are eligible for health insurance benefits, disability benefits and 401(k) benefit plans. The casino also provides revenues to regional governmental entities and provides significant side benefits to the local tourist economy.

Revenues from Michigan Indian gaming reached one billion dollars in 2003, but has remained unchanged from that date, perhaps due to increased competition from gambling operations operated by the state of Michigan and by neighboring states. Gaming has, indeed, boosted the local economy not just for the Grand Traverse Band, but for the entire community. Tribal members receive a yearly stipend from gambling operations in addition to receiving the benefits described by Judge Hillman. At the same time, gaming has not been an unmitigated blessing as gambling addiction has wreaked financial ruin on individuals and families. However, the tribe does not bear sole responsibility for that suffering with the state of Michigan's embrace of the lottery and of gaming in the City of Detroit.

Changes

The growth of Grand Traverse County and stagnant population growth of Traverse City drastically changed the nature of the community. As people become separated from each other geographically, they no longer shopped in the same places, met each other in familiar haunts, attended churches serving close-knit neighborhoods, and sent their children to schools that can be reached by walking or a short bus ride. In the nature of bigness and sprawl there is a concomitant decline in neighborliness.

That is not to say the Traverse area is completely separated into units of function and government that operate independently. Residents of Traverse

City's West Side, East Side, downtown, Garfield Township, East Bay Township, Acme, and Old Mission Peninsula still see themselves as a member of the Traverse area, but they are not as unified as before. West Siders care little about Central High School's success in sports except as it concerns them when they have to play that team. Small businesses downtown do not include hardware stores, department stores, a variety of men's clothing stores, office supply stores, and other outlets utilized by people everywhere. A single large grocery store lies in the center of Traverse City (on Eighth Street) with several at the very outskirts of the city. Most are outside the city limits, serving County residents and City residents willing to drive the distance required to enjoy lower prices. The flow of commerce has largely moved in a direction opposite to that of the past: city dwellers drive outside the city to get the necessaries of life. There is no single, centralized shopping district.

The development of shopping malls outside of town—first Cherryland Mall and then the Grand Traverse Mall—moved the retail center of the region from Front Street to Airport Road skirting the city. "Big Box" stores such as Meijer's and Walmart drew even more shoppers from the central hub of Traverse City. Front Street at present is largely made up of stores designed to appeal to visitors, upper-end women's clothing stores, diverse niche businesses such as a successful store merchandising hats, and a variety of coffee shops and exotic restaurants. Two successful entertainment venues continue, the City Opera House and the State Theater. In addition, residents support two independent bookstores which sponsor frequent cultural events.

Many people wish to live close to the city, both for cultural reasons and to save on transportation costs. As a result, city lots and homes sell for a premium while those ten or twenty miles away increase less in value. Subdivisions often stand with only a few houses built as homebuyers decide to purchase a foreclosed house for thousands less. The outward migration of the population from the city is slowing as people return to the city center. The change reminds us of development patterns before the 1940's.

I will finish this section by interjecting a personal note. From my limited experience interacting with people of this area, I conclude that most people are content with their lives here. To be sure, poverty manifests itself in homelessness, jobs paying no more than minimum wage, and the proliferation of paycheck advance outfits. Traffic can be horrendous by Northern Michigan standards if not by the standards of Chicago or Atlanta. On Old Mission Peninsula ostentatious houses occupy hilltops formerly populated by great white

pines. Long lines outside restaurants in summer do not reflect the Traverse City of years past. Still, in spite of the downsides of increased commerce and development, residents express hope about their city, a hope that manifests itself in many ways: the host of volunteers for the Cherry Festival and the Traverse City Film Festival, the support for public institutions like the Traverse Area District Library, successful millages underwriting public transit, the building of bike trails, and strong backing for Goodwill Industries, the Women's Resource Center, and the Father Fred Foundation. The success of the minor league baseball team, the Traverse City Beach Bums, gives evidence of community solidarity—a shared feeling that we are all in this together. Such attitudes do not last forever: cities decline as well as grow. But at this point in time, Traverse City displays the same spirit it did in 1858.

CHAPTER SIX

Glimpsing the Future

Clinch Park: August, 2043

The Park Place shimmered in the distance as the sun reached its zenith shortly after noon. Just across Grandview Parkway, the Hotel Indigo presented its four-storied façade to Grand Traverse Bay, its guests and local pedestrians taking advantage of an underground walkway, welcoming its coolness as they walked to and from the beach. As it had been all week long, the day would be hot, too hot for sunbathing, too hot for casual conversations in the open, too hot for volleyball on the sandy court nearby. Still, hardy souls did occupy the Open Space, a few dripping with water luxuriously cool from the Bay, a few gathered under the sparse shade of slender maple trees texting and talking, and a single father romping with a toddler oblivious to rosy cheeks, sweat, and breathlessness. Within air-conditioned vehicles, motorists looked out at the park as they sped by on Grandview Parkway, hurrying home or to destinations favored by summer visitors: cabins, motels, camping grounds, and shopping malls. As they passed, they looked beyond the expanse of trees, grass, and people to the Bay beyond: everyone wanted to check its color and the height of the waves that swept in. Of course, it was a mirror to the sky, reflecting the blue when it was clear and the gray when it rained or snowed, but still people gazed—they could not get enough of it—even the locals. It defined Traverse City; it framed it; it connected it to Nature. It was loved for its beauty and feared for its unpredictability. For nearly two hundred years residents had felt that way about their Bay.

Automobiles ran along Grandview Parkway at slower rates than formerly, pedestrian crossings at intersections interrupting their hurry. Most of them were electric, drivers having converted from gasoline during a price spike that raised the cost of a gallon of gasoline to the cost of a lunch at a local diner. Buses fueled by natural gas brought visitors to the area, many of whom would promptly become drivers, renting electric cars—some comically small—to travel to Sleeping Bear Dunes, Old Mission, golf courses, swimming holes, fishing spots, and sundry places around town. The noise and smells of internal combustion engines were diminished when compared to this place thirty years ago: It was a welcome change.

A large passenger boat had docked in front of the Maritime Academy, its passengers disembarking as a merry throng, their voices reflecting the many lands they came from: China, Germany, Japan, Brazil, and the Middle East. Rapidly they scattered to board tour buses, hire taxis, and to begin shopping adventures on foot, always inspecting their internet devices to determine directions, the best restaurants, and the way to the nearest restroom. While Traverse City had not become significantly more diverse in its year-around population, it had begun to attract the world's people during the summer season. That change had stimulated an economy which had done very well in recent years even without the brisk trade of summer. As the density of population had increased with the building of apartments and condos close to the downtown hub, stores, restaurants, and entertainment venues had prospered apace. There was talk about how Traverse City was becoming a small version of Santa Fe or Boulder in its attractiveness to young people with money to spend, but then—that talk had been going around for decades. Underneath it all, it wasn't true: the city was what it was—a small town, now grown to a middle-sized one, comprised of people who wanted to live in a place isolated from the larger currents stirring world events, a place situated at the end of a long peninsula.

Looking Forward: 2043

Inevitably the historian reaches the present in his telling of the past, but still he is not done—since he is confronted by the question, "What next?" Following the trajectories of past, what direction is history pointing—at least within the limited foresight of the near future? Here his job becomes easier at least in one respect: He does not have to pay as much attention to facts and can let his imagination roam freely.

Some changes to come are certain. For example, the climate is warming world-wide and the impacts of that warming will be felt locally in many ways. The Bay will recede as the water lowers through increased evaporation and warmer temperatures. East Bay, with a vast area of shallow water near shore will become a sandy beach extending from the present shore a third to a half mile in places. Snow in winter will become uncertain, the snowpack often melting off completely before returning again and again. Skiing, snowboarding, and snowmobiling will be affected by winters more characteristic of Kentucky than Northern Michigan. At the same time, wetlands will disappear as the water table drops, causing local extinction of certain orchids, insectivorous plants, and examples of boreal (northern) species at the southern edge of their distribution.

The forest landscape will change as a consequence of the great warming. Some tree species, formerly important, will mostly disappear from the biota as disease, invasive plants, and pests arrive from other lands. Already the American Chestnut and the American Elm have been removed as components of natural ecosystems because of Chestnut Blight and Dutch Elm disease respectively. At present, White Ash is dying because of the onslaught of Emerald Ash Borer. Parenthetically, it might be mentioned that morel mushrooms are forecast to diminish as the ash disappears since a definite association has been noticed between the two species.

The American Beech is in trouble because of Beech Scale disease and will decline as a member of the upland Northern Michigan hardwoods ecosystem. Animals that survived on beechnuts will be adversely affected by its demise. The American Hemlock is being attacked by Wooly Adelgids, aphid-like insects that cause early death of the trees. At the same time, Oak Wilt attacks many species of oaks, threatening this important component of the forest. The forests of the future will be different from those we now enjoy.

Natural landscapes today would not be recognized by settlers of Grand Traverse a hundred years ago. South of Silver Lake Road near Meijer's, the wetlands are covered with invasive Common Buckthorn, an aggressive small tree that forms an impenetrable thicket. The 1850 survey of the region indicates that spruce, white cedar, American elm, and American hemlock occupied this area at that time. Opening the land for grazing lowered the water table and made it possible for the aggressive buckthorn to invade. The pristine sand dunes of Sleeping Bear are fighting an infestation of Baby's Breath, a European weed that breaks off and forms "tumbleweeds" that spread their seeds upon the sand. Under the hardwood forest canopy spring wildflowers are yielding to Myrtle and Sweet Woodruff as Trillium, Adder's Tongue, and Dutchman's Breeches become harder to find. In the next hundred years the flora and fauna would appear as foreign to us as the present landscape would appear to early settlers.

Climate change will affect local agriculture, too. One effect of global warming is the occurrence of unpredictable and unexpected warm spells during early spring. One such event occurred in 2012 which resulted in the destruction of the cherry crop for that year. Such crop failures will become more common in the future, possibly ending the area's dominance in the tart cherry industry. Oregon, being closer to the stabilizing influence of the Pacific Ocean, will take up the slack as cherry production declines in Michigan.

The effects of climate change and the spread of invasive species have already been felt throughout the Great Lakes, both locally and regionally. The invasion of the Sea Lamprey caused the decline of Lake Trout—which resulted in the stocking of Pacific Salmon as the chief predator. Alewives replaced native Lake Herring at the bottom of the food chain. Zebra and Quagga mussels entered the Great Lakes in the ballast of international vessels, disrupting the ecosystem food chains in unpredicted ways. Recently hundreds of Common Loons died as a result of eating fish contaminated with botulism, a disease that developed as a consequence of the growth of algae and the availability of nutrients. Quagga mussels have been implicated as an important factor in promoting algae growth. There is no doubt that other invasive organisms are waiting backstage to make their appearance in Lake Michigan and Lake Huron. The dreaded Asian Carp is one of those bad actors threatening the prosperity of the Great Lakes fishery.

What about the unexpected effects of global warming—the "unknown unknowns"? Will increased prices for corn result in deforestation of the region as corn fields replace trees? Will the presence of fresh water in the Great Lakes trigger an immigration of human beings seeking the benefits of that resource? Will heat waves in the Midwest send tourists to the north in droves, running from weeks of hundred-degree heat to the relative ninety-degree coolness of Northern Michigan? These questions cannot be answered with certainty— the trajectories of past events are not clearly established, making prediction difficult. We must be nearer that future to make good guesses.

The same thinking applies to changes in the human population of the Traverse area: we cannot predict who will come and who will go. Compared to many areas of the United States, Traverse City shows little diversity in ethnicity, race, religion, or politics. It is mostly white, Western European, Christian, and Republican—as it has always been. The reason for this constancy boils down to an absence of causes triggering change. Heavy industry did not beckon Southern blacks to build better lives here; a warm climate and good soil did not encourage Hispanics to come this far north to make farms; geographic isolation—as well as media isolation—kept the area free of settlers and migrants for many years. The area had no minerals to mine, no more untouched forests to cut. It stayed the same out of inertia: a body at rest stays at rest.

That is not to say Traverse City stayed aloof from the twentieth and twenty-first centuries. The KKK does not command the attention and popularity it did in the 1920's. Unlike the early times, women participate in business and public affairs, taking leadership roles in many fields. The natural environment is treasured by all citizens now—perhaps as atonement for the atrocities committed a hundred years ago. And the poor and "insane" are treated far differently now as contrasted to the days of poor houses and asylums. The city has become modern.

As it has become modern, it drank in the poisons of modern culture along with the goodness: omnipresent joblessness, jobs unable to support families, poverty for those crushed by debt, the end of neighborliness with the construction of large condo and apartment units, the decline of public institutions, and the fracturing of the community along political, religious, and cultural lines. During the Great Recession of 2007-8, the unemployment rate of Grand Traverse County reached 14 percent, a figure comparable to that of the state generally. Like all of Michigan, the Traverse area is vulnerable to economic devastation whenever the nation's economy collapses.

In the past, wages in the Traverse area have been significantly lower than those of Southern Michigan, but with the reduction in auto manufacturing, that difference may be less now. Here and everywhere in Michigan unskilled workers take on two or three jobs at near-minimum wage just to pay the bills. The Traverse area workforce is not unionized for the most part, the local population holding negative views towards unions. Historically, resort, restaurant, and retail businesses pay notoriously low wages as compared to skilled manufacturing. The local economy has few of those desirable, higher-paying jobs. According to the 2000 census the median family income of Traverse City residents was slightly below the national median, while that of Grand Traverse residents was roughly the same as that number. There is no reason to think that family incomes will soar in years to come: Traverse City will remain a middle-class town.

One possible source of income may be developed locally: fracking underground deposits to obtain natural gas. While there is some resistance to the practice from environmentalists, the area is strongly supportive of the fossil fuel extraction and is unlikely to forbid fracking operations. The economic and environmental effects of such natural gas extraction are not clear. Certainly the collision of values between locals' love of Nature and their love of economic gain will result in dissension and vigorous debate.

Like the nation as a whole, the Grand Traverse area is splintered into religious and political factions. These fractures play out in the choice of media, in K-12 schools, and in elected officials sent to Lansing and Washington. WTCM, formerly a community radio station uncommitted to political ideology, has become an outlet for right-wing talk radio. The local newspaper, the *Record-Eagle*, trends toward Democrats in its political endorsements, though it attempts to steer a middle course generally. Competing "free" newspapers such as the *Grand Traverse Insider* present a more conservative point of view, while the popular *Northern Express* is decidedly left.

Ten years ago the Traverse City Area Public Schools, Pathfinder School, St. Francis, and scattered religious and private schools offered educational choices to parents. Now, with the advent of Traverse City Christian School and charter schools such as the Grand Traverse Academy, large numbers of students are educated in separate institutions each with its own sports teams, musical events, and student plays and activities. The public schools and St. Francis are not the uniting forces in the community that they used to be.

Politically the area is divided, too. The City of Traverse City votes Democratic in presidential elections on occasion, but Grand Traverse County continues to vote overwhelmingly Republican. Among Republicans there is a split between strongly conservative "Tea Party" adherents and more moderate mainstream candidates. In the state Senate race in the district comprising Leelanau, Benzie, and Manistee Counties, a strongly conservative candidate edged out the Democrat by only a few hundred votes in the 2012 election. The stark division between political attitudes is demonstrated by the close race.

Politically, there is no reason to think the area will change. It will remain a conservative stronghold largely because of demographics. Whites will continue to dominate locally in a nation where minorities are growing in numbers and influence, making the area out of step with national trends. At the same time, as it has in the past, the city of Traverse City itself will break away from Northern Michigan in occasionally supporting candidates and issues from the left.

Increases in the price of fuel will cause residents to think twice about building homes many miles from their jobs. In an age of cheap gasoline, there was no penalty for settling ten or twenty miles from Traverse City. In fact, lower property taxes easily made up the difference in expenses. In the future, those savings will evaporate, resulting in more desirable building places closer to town—if not within the city limits. Bicycle transportation, both for recreation and for commuting, is more practical near population centers rather than far away from the city hub. A fine network of bike paths extending outward from the city beckons bicyclists in the warmer months of the year—and for a few brave souls—even in the blast of winter.

Unlike some cities, Traverse City does not depend upon a few local philanthropists to accomplish civic and cultural goals. It does not have the Dow family as Midland does, the Upjohn Company as Kalamazoo does, the Ford Company as Detroit does, or the Mott family as Flint does. The public broadcasting outlet WIAA depends primarily upon its listeners for support, the City Opera House collects donations from a variety of sources, and institutions serving the poor survive through grants and relatively modest gifts from a cross-section of the population.

That is not to say philanthropy on a large scale does not exist: Mike Dennos and his wife Barbara were mostly responsible for the Dennos Art Museum; Rotary Charities—fortunate to have gas and oil revenue pouring in from property it owns—makes sizable contributions to a variety of worthy causes; the Les Biederman and Gerald Oleson Foundations fund a variety of nonprofits in the community; and the Grand Traverse Band of Ottawa and Chippewa Indians donates to causes that benefit not only tribal members but all of the people of the area. In addition to these sources the City of Traverse City receives royalties from gas discovered on its Brown Bridge property. It spends interest on the principal to lower city taxes.

The largess obtained through individuals and foundations is not sufficient to fund the worthy projects underway in the city. Ordinary people contribute time and money to make things happen; maintaining the TART trail, clearing trash out of the Boardman River, volunteering as docents for the Land Conservancy or the Dennos Museum, or helping with various athletic events from bicycle races to marathons. During its entire existence the community has demonstrated a spirit of giving back. In the future it will continue as newcomers follow the pattern set by those who came first. In that sense, the history of the community lives on.

The future is a vast and limitless place. While the near-future—the next thirty or forty years—can be glimpsed in blurred image, the far-future lies in impenetrable fog. Fifty years ago, who could have guessed how the internet would change American life? In 1890, who would have predicted the effect of the auto on American society? Radio, television, the movies—all appeared abruptly with little foreshadowing of their coming. So it is with us now. Prediction of the far-future is futile since we cannot capture the insignificant traces that point to major change.

Some things will remain nearly constant, though: the lay of the land, the rush of the Boardman River, and the tumble of waves upon the shore of the Bay. In photographs from the 1890's we see the same hills, the same valleys, the same waters. A hundred years from now our descendants will recognize them still. As the first settlers went down to the Bay in 1858—perhaps to see a comet, perhaps to look out on the water—so will people do the same a hundred years from now. It would be well if they would remember us now and all those who came before—how we made our lives in this beautiful and isolated place.

Notable Events in the Grand Traverse Area, 1847-2013

1847-1860

1847: Horace Boardman establishes sawmill at Mill Creek (Kids Creek)

1851: Perry Hannah arrives in the Traverse area

1858: *Grand Traverse Herald* begins publication

1869: Northport-Newaygo road completed

1869: Ladies Library founded

1870-1879

1873: Railroad service begins in Traverse City, Telegraph arrives

1877: First St. Francis school built

1877: First school at site of present Central Elementary opens

1880-1889

1883: Hannah and Lay brick building opens at Front and Union

1885: Northern Michigan Asylum opens

1889: First steam-powered electric power plant on West Bay begins operations

1889: Visitors gather at Edgewood Resort

1890-1899

1892: City Opera House opens

1894: Steinberg's Opera House opens

1894: Boardman River Light and Power builds Boardman dam

1894: Oval Wood Dish Company moves to Traverse City

1898: Flood devastates west side of Traverse City

1900-1909

1900: County Courthouse is built

1902: Front Street paved between Union and Cass Streets

1904: Perry Hannah dies

1905: Public Library opens on Sixth Street

1910-1919

1911: *Traverse City Record-Eagle* begins publication

1912: Traverse City Light and Power founded

1915: Dixie Highway opens, east and west branches

1915: First Munson Hospital, corner of Eleventh and Elmwood founded

1917: Oval Wood Dish leaves town

1917: Interlochen State Park created

1919: Labor unrest strikes at several local businesses

1920-1929

1920: Traverse City State Park (now, Keith Charters) created

1924: KKK bombing behind Lyric Theater

1925: Brick hospital built upon present Munson Hospital site

1925: "Blessing of the Blossoms," the beginning of the National Cherry Festival held on Old Mission Peninsula for the first time

1926: First airport constructed on Ransom Hill off Veterans Drive

1928: First National Music Camp opens

1929: Park Place ten-story building is completed

1930-1939

1930: Steamship service to Chicago ends

1931: Bond passed to build sewage treatment plant

1931: Clinch Park (clean-up) created through citizen efforts

1934: Central High School destroyed by fire

1934: City issues scrip to pay workers

1937: Hugh J. Gray cairn completed at Kewadin

1938: Cherry Capitol Airport begins passenger service

1940-49

1940: City Manager plan of city governance adopted

1941: First local radio station, WTCM (580) begins broadcasting

1943: Migrants from Jamaica and Mexico arrive to harvest cherries

1948: John T. Parsons and Frank Stulen develop numerical control

1950-1959

1951: First Northwestern Michigan College classes meet at airport

1952: Traverse Symphony Orchestra begins

1953: Grandview Parkway built

1954: Northern Michigan's first TV station, WPBN goes on the air

1955: Northwestern Michigan College moves to Front Street campus

1955: Cherry County Playhouse begins

1959: Central High School moves to Milliken Avenue

1960-1969

1960: Traverse City Civic Players (later, Old Town Playhouse) stages first play

1963: Interlochen Arts Academy opens

1963: WIAA (Interlochen Public Radio) begins broadcasting

1968-70 Mechanical cherry harvesters arrive; migrant numbers decline

1970-1979

1970: Legislation authorizing Sleeping Bear Dunes National Lakeshore is signed

1970: School consolidation: Traverse City Junior High opens on West Silver Lake Road

1974: Chateau Grand Traverse Vineyard on Old Mission Peninsula opens

1975 Boskydel Vineyard on Leelanau Peninsula opens

1978: Cherryland Mall opens

1979: Downtown Development Authority (DDA) created

1979: Judge Noel Fox affirms Treaty of 1836 fishing and hunting rights

1980-1989

1980: Grand Traverse Band of Ottawa and Chippewa Indians achieves tribal recognition

1981: Grand Traverse County Courthouse rededicated

1985: Leelanau Sands Casino begins operations

1985: Munson becomes a regional healthcare provider: Munson Healthcare

1989: Traverse City Regional Psychiatric Hospital (Traverse City State Hospital) closes

1990-1999

1991: Dennos Museum opens on NMC campus

1992: Grand Traverse Mall opens

1996: Turtle Creek Casino opens

1997: West Senior High School opens in township

1998: New library is constructed at Woodmere location

1998: Traverse Area Recreational Trail (TART) established

2000-2013

2004: New terminal at Cherry Capitol Airport in completed

2005: Traverse City Film Festival is celebrated for the first time

2006: Traverse City *Beach Bums* baseball team is organized

2009: First National Writers Series is inaugurated

2012: Brown Bridge Dam removed as part of Boardman River restoration

2013: Con Foster Museum becomes a community movie theater

2013: Construction begins on Hotel Indigo

Aerial Photographs of the Grand Traverse Area

c. 1925

Aerial photo of Traverse City looking south towards Boardman Lake. At left center are the railway yards and roundhouse of the west shore of the lake. Left to right is Park Street (no bridge) and Cass Street. At the right hand side, slightly above center, is the empty land that would soon become Thirlby Field.

c. 1935

State Hospital looking west

c. 1940s

West Bay from the stack of the power plant, east to Oak Street and beyond. The main east-west road in the photograph is West Front Street.

c. 1960

Aerial view of the Front Street business area looking east. The intersection of Front and Union Street is in the center of the image. Starting on the north-west corner of that intersection you can see the Traverse City State Bank (now 5th/3rd), the Hannah Lay building, the Masonic Building and the Wilhelm Building. Since this photo was taken, both the Masonic and Wilhelm buildings suffered fires that led to their top floors being demolished.

Late 1940s

Central neighborhood, note Center High School in center of photograph.

c. 1940

Aerial view, looking southeast, of the Traverse City waterfront. The Park Place Hotel can be seen in the upper right hand corner of the image, the bottom right hand corner shows the John D. Morgan Co. canning facility. Quite small, in the middle of the photo, are the Elsie Hannah Bathhouse and Con Foster Museum. The museum building still graces the bay front, and plans are underway for the Traverse City Film Festival to turn it into a small movie theater.

c. 1940

Aerial view of downtown Traverse City and West Bay, looking east. Con Foster Museum and Clinch Park can be seen on the left in the middle of the page, but Grandview Parkway has not been built. A parade can be seen on Front Street, to the right.

c. 1945

Aerial view of the racetrack at the Northwestern Michigan Fairgrounds on East Front Street, now the Grand Traverse County Civic Center. That track ran east and west, whereas the present day walking trail runs north and south.

c. 1945

Photo by Al Barnes, looking north. Today the large building in the middle is Cone Drive on 12th Street. The church towards the top left is the old St. Francis building on the corner of 10th and Cass. On the right of the image are the rail yards that occupied the west side of Boardman Lake.

c. 1945

Aerial view, looking north, of the intersection of East Front and Railroad Avenue. The mouth of the Boardman River is at the top of the photo. When Grandview Parkway was built in the early 1950s, the mouth of the river was moved westward. Today the Holiday Inn sits near the river's original mouth, close to the location of the houses in the upper right hand corner of the photo.

c. 1950s

Grandview Parkway soon after completion. The Cass Street and Park Street bridges cross the Boardman River.

c. 1950

Aerial view looking north up Union towards the bay. The Post Office at State and Union is in the bottom left of the image. About two-thirds of the way up, center, at the intersection of Front and Union, one can see the Traverse City State Bank (today 5th/3rd), and the Hannah Lay building. Directly across to the south are the Wilhelm Building on the left, and the Masonic building on the right. Both buildings still stand today, but have lost upper floors to fires.

c.1957

Aerial photo looking a bit south of due east. The street running across the bottom of the image is Division Street. The intersection in the lower right hand corner shows Division, 14th Street and the east end of what is now Silver Lake Road. To the left of center you can see Thirlby Field just north of 14th. The ice-covered body of water at the end of 14th Street is Boardman Lake.

Mid-twentieth century

Aerial of Munson Hospital, looking west. The empty lot on the bottom left had long been used for recreational activities such as football and baseball. Today it is the Munson parking lot. The main Munson building was never demolished. What we currently see as the Munson Medical Center complex was built up around this original building.

Resource Guide

I will not present a formal bibliography for this work, but will list sources helpful to me and helpful for all researchers studying the history of Traverse City and Grand Traverse County. Reference librarians and other officials can provide further information about availability and loan policies. Genealogical research aids are not described here.

Indexes

Essential to all local research is the *Traverse City Newspaper Index* compiled by Lucille Zoulek and Helen Langworthy. Covering the years 1858 to 1977 (later extended to 1985), it lists article topics from the *Grand Traverse Herald, The Traverse Bay Eagle, The Evening Record,* and the *Traverse City Record-Eagle* (see below). This index is found at the Reference Desk of the Traverse Area District Library (TADL), at the Archives of the History Center of Traverse City, and at the Northwestern Michigan College library. It may be found online at https://dspace.nmc.edu/handle/11045/22872.

Another index of interest to those studying nineteenth century local history is Bob Wilson's *Index to News Items 1858-1899,* a work that includes news items ordered chronologically and arranged by topic from the *Grand Traverse Herald.* Researchers may ask for it at the TADL reference desk and the History Center Archives.

Two reference works—not exactly indexes—are useful for those studying businesses located along Front Street: the *Traverse City Central Business Survey,* 1977 assembled by the Historic District Commission, and Marie Scott's *Front Street Survey,* 1992. Both are located at the TADL reference desk.

City Directories

The *Polk Directory* gives information about residents and businesses of Traverse City between the years 1900 up to modern times. Both TADL and the History Center possess a collection of these valuable research aids, though a few volumes are missing at each location. An early city directory, F.E. Walker's *City Directory* (1898) exists in photocopied form at the library and the History Center. In addition, the public library has telephone directories from as early as the 1940's (with many years missing).

Traverse City is unusual among cities in that it has a lineage of newspapers that begins before the Civil War and extends to the present day. The *Grand Traverse Herald* commenced printing in 1858, that company giving birth to *The Morning Record, Evening Record*, and eventually to the *Traverse City Record-Eagle*. The *Bay Eagle* started as an independent newspaper but merged with the *Evening Record* to form the *Record-Eagle*. Copies exist in microfilm at Northwestern Michigan College and at the Public Library for all of them, so a significant number of *Evening Record's* are missing from the year 1915. The History Center has a large number of bound newspapers, the *Herald, Evening Record*, and the *Record-Eagle* covering a long span of time beginning in the nineteenth century and ending in the forties. That collection features approximately thirty issues of the *Evening Record* not displayed on microfilm. In addition, both NMC and the public libraries has scattered copies of the *Traverse City News* and *Honest Opinion*, a socialist newspaper published just after World War I.

Beginning in May, 2013 the TADL will offer access through its website to all local newspapers from the earliest edition of the *Herald* to the *Traverse City Record-Eagle* (years up to 1977, 1988-89) with compete coverage to the present day promised in the near future. This service will be free of charge to all library cardholders living within the Traverse Area District Library boundaries. An advantage to using this resource is that stored issues are searchable by keywords, a feature that can save the researcher much time. The convenience of conducting research from home is an additional benefit.

MAPS AND CITY/COUNTY DOCUMENTS

The public library and the History Center possess plat maps in paper form, 1881, 1895, and 1908 the earliest years available. Minutes of the City Commission exist in paper at the public library and in microfiche at the Traverse City City Clerk's office at the Governmental Center. Planning documents dating from Traverse City's earliest plan (1942) can be examined at the City Planning Department in that building.

PHOTOGRAPHS

The History Center of Traverse City has an extensive collection of historical photographs which may be examined online at http://grandtraverse.past-perfect-online.com/Blank_1.html. The Traverse Area Public Library has the

Floyd Webster Historical Photograph Collection, a collection of postcards and photographs of the Kingsley area primarily. It may be accessed online at localhistory.tadl.org. *Grand Traverse: Reflections Along the Bay,* a book published by the *Record-Eagle,* contains numerous photos of the area.

School Yearbooks

The following institutions have nearly complete collections of yearbooks for Traverse City Central High School: TADL, the History Center, Traverse City Central Library. Collections begin in the year 1900. TADL also has yearbooks from Kingsley, St. Francis, the Grant Traverse Academy, and Traverse City Christian High School.

Hannah and Lay Records

The Bentley Historical Library of the University of Michigan owns a large collection of Hannah and Lay records. Researchers can make arrangements to examine the collection by email or telephone.

Local Periodicals

TADL has back issues of *Reflections by the Bays* (later, *Grand Traverse Scene*) and *Traverse: The Magazine* both of which feature occasional articles about Traverse area history. The History Center of Traverse City has a complete collection of the *Preview*, a weekly newspaper that often had articles about local history.

Traverse City State Hospital (Northern Michigan Asylum)
Reports to the State of Michigan

TADL and the History Center hold a collection of paper documents dating from 1883 related to the State Hospital. The reports are focused on institutional data, not individual patient records.

Early Histories

M.L. Leach's *History of Grand Traverse and Leelanau Counties* (1883), originally published as a series in the *Grand Traverse Herald*, presents interesting material about Northwestern Lower Michigan especially concerning the first pioneers and tales of Indian life. Its commentary about the Beaver Island Mormons is flawed, however, since it is based upon biased accounts taken from newspapers and memories of anti-Mormon settlers. Lavishly illustrated with many fine portraits, landscapes, and views of buildings, *The Traverse Region, Historical and Descriptive* (1884), largely derived from Leach's work, tells the history of nine Northwestern Michigan counties. A somewhat later history, *Sprague's History of Grand Traverse and Leelanau Counties* (1903) covers much of the same ground as Leach. All three books may be borrowed from TADL and Northwestern Michigan College.

LATER HISTORICAL WORKS

Newspaperman Al Barnes wrote many delightful books concerning local history: *Vinegar Pie and Other Tales, Supper in the Evening,* and *Let's Fly Backward* to name three. Following in his footsteps, Larry Wakefield explored many aspects of Traverse history, his important titles being *Rail and Sail: A Narrative History of Transportation in the Traverse City Region* (1980); *Historic Traverse City Houses; The Way It Was: Stories from the Grand Traverse Region; All Our Yesterdays: A Narrative History of Traverse City and the Region;* and *Queen City of the North: An Illustrated History of Traverse City from Its Beginnings to the 1980s.* In his three volume *Grand Traverse Legends* (2004, 2005, 2006), Robert Wilson assembled a marvelous collection of biographies of notable nineteenth century Traverse area residents. Finally, the author of this book has written three books (2008, 2009, 2011) focusing on issues such as labor conflict, poverty, racism, the position of women, crime and punishment: *Glimpses of Grand Traverse Past; Who We Were, What We Did: Fresh Perspectives on Grand Traverse History;* and *Gateways to Grand Traverse Past.* All books may be obtained from local libraries.

SOURCES ABOUT THE STATE OF MICHIGAN

The *Michigan Manual,* published yearly or semi-annually since 1867, offers a wealth of information concerning demographics, election results, natural resources, taxation, economics, and history. To gain a statewide perspective on history, I turn to historian Willis F. Dunbar's *Michigan: A History of the Wolverine State,* first published in 1965, updated in 1995.

In this age of the Internet, it is possible to read historical works out of copyright in the comfort of one's home. For example, Google Books lets us examine Leach's *History of Grand Traverse and Leelanau Counties* without the inconvenience of entering a library door. In addition to old works, some websites honor the history of the institution they represent with extensive information about its history. The following sites proved valuable to me in writing this book:

Traverse City Downtown Development Authority
downtowntc.com/about-us

Traverse City Cherry Festival
cherryfestival.org

Traverse City Film Festival
traversecityfilmfest.org/festival-basics

Munson Medical Center
munsonhealthcare.org/history

Northwestern Michigan College
nmc.edu/about/history-archives

Traverse Symphony Orchestra
traversesymphony.org

Old Town Playhouse
oldtownplayhouse.com/history

Interlochen Center for the Arts
interlochen.org/content/history

Sleeping Bear Dunes National Lakeshore
nps.gov/slbe/historyculture

Across Grandview Parkway: Strengthening Connections Between Downtown and the Bay: A project submitted in partial fulfillment for the degrees of Mater of Landscape Architecture, at the University of Michigan's School of Natural Resources and Environment, and for the degree of Master of Urban Planning from the Taubman College of Architecture and Urban Planning, April 2006. Authors: Erik Dayrell, Lisa DuRussel, Leah Hollstein, Sabrina Siebert, and Lindsay Smith, University of Michigan

Boal, Dean, *Interlochen, Home of the Arts,* Ann Arbor: University of Michigan Press, 1998

Biederman, Lester, (edited by Nancy Baxter), *Happy Days: An Autobiography,* Traverse City, MI: Pioneer Study Press, 1982

Catton, Bruce, *Waiting for the Morning Train,* Detroit, Wayne State University Press, 1987

Decker, William A, *Northern Michigan Asylum: A History of the Traverse City State Hospital,* 2010: Traverse City, MI, 2010

Fletcher, Matthew, *The Eagle Returns: The Legal History of the Grand Traverse Band of Ottawa and Chippewa Indians,* East Lansing: Michigan State University Press, 2012

Karamanski, Theodore, *A Nationalized Lakeshore: The Creation and Administration of Sleeping Bear Dunes National Lakeshore,* Midwest Regional Office, National Park Service, United States Department of the Interior, Omaha., 2000

Tanis, Preston, *Northwestern Michigan: The First Twenty Years,* March, 1973

Shumsky, Al, *Northwestern Michigan College: The Second Twenty Years,* 1971-1991, February, 1994

Weeks, George, *Mem-ka-weh: Dawning of the Grand Traverse Band of Ottawa and Chippewa Indians,* Grand Traverse Band of Ottawa and Chippewa Indians, Traverse City: Village Press, 1992

Made in the USA
Middletown, DE
12 June 2024

55638118R00080